CONFEDERATE RECORDS

FROM THE

ELBERT COUNTY, GEORGIA, COURT OF ORDINARY

1890 - 1932

By
Michael A. Ports

CLEARFIELD

Printed for Clearfield Company by
Genealogical Publishing Company
Baltimore, Maryland
2016

ISBN 978-0-8063-5802-4

Made in the United States of America

Table of Contents

3

Introduction

The following transcriptions include all of the Confederate records contained on the microfilm roll prepared by the Genealogical Society of Salt Lake City, Utah, in cooperation with the Georgia Department of Archives and History, in Morrow, Georgia. The microfilm was made in the Office of the ordinary at Elberton in 1960. The heading on the microfilm roll reads

Elbert County
State of Georgia
Court of Ordinary
Pension Rolls
Book 1821-1923
Index

The microfilm roll appears to contain four separate volumes of original records, each of which is transcribed here in the order that they appear on the microfilm roll. The first volume has the title *Widows Pension Dots.* on the outside front cover, the second and third volumes both are titled *Pension Record*, and the fourth volume is titled *Pension Roll of Elbert County*. For the most part, all four volumes consist of pre-printed forms in a tabular format intended to document the pension payments made by the County Ordinary to each veteran or widow. The original record volumes occasionally include additional material, including one muster roll, correspondence, and a certificate. While the heading on the microfilm roll indicates differently, the actual pension records cover the period from 1890 through 1932.

While some of the information also is available in the compiled military service records at the National Archives and Records Administration in Washington, DC and widely available on microfilm and the internet, as well as the pension application files held by the Georgia Department of Archives and History, much of the information is available nowhere else. For example, many of the compiled military service records are incomplete or nonexistent, whereas the following muster and pension rolls contain detailed information on the soldier's military service, such as date and place of enlistment, date and place of wounds, date and place of capture, place of confinement, date of exchange, location and service at the close of the war, date and cause for discharge, and length of residence in Elbert County. In a few cases, the date for the start of residence in the county is the veteran's or widow's birth date. The pension rolls often include the date and place of birth or the date of death for the veterans and widows, many of whom died before 1919, when Georgia began recording death certificates. In addition, the widows pension rolls often include a date and place of marriage.

The original records include both typewritten, printed, and handwritten records. For the most part, the handwriting is legible, making transcription a fairly straightforward process. However, because of occasional ink blots and smudges, torn pages, as well as imperfections of the microfilm, individual words could not be deciphered, such occasions noted with brackets, for

4

example [smudge] or [illegible]. The use of three consecutive underscores, i. e. ___, indicates a blank space where the clerk never entered the information on the record. The transcriptions of the muster and pension rolls presents dates in a standardized format, spells out most abbreviated place names, corrects incorrectly spelled place names, and corrects grammar and punctuation. No attempt is made to correct the spellings of any names, no matter how obvious the error. Researchers should consult the microfilm or even the original records to formulate alternative interpretations.

In addition, military units are presented in a standard format. For example, 38 Ga means the 38th Regiment Georgia Infantry and 1 SC Rifles means 1st Regiment South Carolina Rifles. The transcription spells out the designations artillery and cavalry, but omits the designation infantry. In a similar manner, designations such as battery, battalion, legion, and reserves are spelled out and the designation regiment is omitted. While by far most of the veterans served in units raised in Elbert County or elsewhere in Georgia, veterans of units raised in Alabama, Kentucky, Missouri, North Carolina, South Carolina, and Tennessee moved to Elbert County after the war.

The book is dedicated to the memory of all of the Confederate veterans from Elbert County who served honorably during the war, especially those who suffered in northern prisons or who were disabled. A review of the extant federal census schedules reveals that virtually every able bodied male resident of Elbert County of military age served in the Confederate army. Many thanks are due the very kind, helpful, and knowledgeable staff at the Georgia Department of Archives and History, who assisted in locating and understanding the context of the records. Thanks also are due Joe Garonzik, of the Genealogical Publishing Company, for his professional advice and counsel. Special thanks are offered to Marcia Tremonti for her encouragement and patience during this challenging endeavor.

Volume I

On the outside cover of the first volume, the clerk wrote *Widows Pension Dots*. On the inside cover, the clerk wrote

> Dear Mrs. L. A. Colvard
>   " Mary T. House
>   " Sallie Haynes

On the first page of the volume, the clerk again wrote *"Widows Pension Dots."* The volume contains a partial index that is not included here. In spite of its title, the volume includes entries for both widows and for soldiers, apparently all pensioners. The individual undated entries consist of the pensioner's name, name of the widow's husband, the company and regiment or other unit in which he served, when he enlisted, when he was discharged or died, year of marriage, and how long the pensioner lived in Elbert County. Occasionally, the entry includes additional details. A typical entry appears below.

The following transcription presents the relevant information in a tabular format with six columns, namely the name of the widow, the name of her soldier husband, the company and regiment or other unit in which he served, remarks, and the page number of the original volume on which the entry appears. The remarks column includes all of the other information contained in the entry.

List of Pensioners

Widow	Husband	Co	Regiment	Remarks	Page
Mrs. P. E. Brown	Asa C. Brown	F	38 Ga	Entered service May 1862. Entered battle Wilderness, 5 May 1864 and shot dead on field. Lived in County since 1836. Married 1851.	3
Mrs. Mary E. Cunningham	Thos. C. Cunningham	G	37 Ga	Entered service Mar 1862. Served until 28 May 1862, when died from attack of measles. Lived in County since 1837. Married 1857.	3
Mrs. Lucy A. Colvard	John H. Colvard	D	1 Ga Reserves	Entered service Jun 1863. Served until 7 Sep 1863, when died of brain fever. Lived in County since 1824. Married 1838.	5
Mrs. Ann H. Dye	Joseph B. Dye		9 Ga Battalion	Transferred to an artillery company 1863, went west, entered battle Bakers Creek, Mississippi, and never heard from again. Lived in County since 4 Oct 1824. Married 1841. Wilkes County	5
Mrs. Julia A. Ginn	James A. Ginn	H	38 Ga	Entered service Aug 1862. Shot dead on battlefield at 2nd Manassas 30	7

Widow	Husband	Co	Regiment	Remarks	Page
				or 31 Aug 1862. Lived in County since 14 Jan 1837. Married 1858.	
Mrs. Marsted A. Hewell	W. W. Hewell	D	10 Ga	Entered service Apr 1863. Died 15 Aug 1863 from diarrhea contracted in the service at Gordonsville, Virginia. Lived in County since 1834. Married 1853.	7
Mrs. Lizzie Jones	W. G. B. Jones	G	37 Ga	Entered service May 1862. Died 17 Dec 1862 from sickness contracted in the service. Lived in County since 17 Oct 1833. Married 1857.	9
Mrs. Eurrene M. Mattox	William D. Mattox	B	1 Ga Reserves	Entered service May 1864. Served until he died Oct 1864 from sickness contracted in the service. Lived in County since 1819. Married 1837.	9
Mrs. Sarah Moon	Jacob D. Moon	E	2 Ga Battalion Sharp Shooters	Entered service Sep 1863. Went into battle Kennesaw Mountain, Georgia 22 Jun 1864, mortally wounded, and died 28 Jun 1864. Lived in County since 1827.	11

Widow	Husband	Co	Regiment	Remarks	Page
				Married 1846.	
Mrs. D. A. Pulliam	Nathan Pulliam	H	38 Ga	Entered service 1862. Contracted a severe sickness from which he remained in bed until he died 15 Jun 1865. Lived in County since 1837. Married 1857.	11
Mrs. R. J. Sorrow	S. P. Sorrow	C	15 Ga	Entered service Jul 1861. While in service at Culpepper Court House, Virginia, taken sick and died 28 Nov 1861. Lived in County since 1827. Married 1845.	13
Mrs. Mary A. Sanders	Jacob E. Sanders	H	38 Ga	Entered service 1861. Served until Jul 1863, when shot dead at battle Gettysburg. Lived in County since 1841. Married 1860.	13
Mrs. Lucinda A. Thornton	William T. Thornton	F	38 Ga	Entered service Aug or Sep 1862. Entered battle Fredericksburg, Virginia, and shot through face and head, died 29 Jan 1863. Lived in County since 29 Oct 1831. Married 1852.	15

Widow	Husband	Co	Regiment	Remarks	Page
Mrs. Martha J. Vaughn	Jacob D. Vaughn	H	38 Ga	Entered service 1861. died 31 May 1862 from congestive chill contracted in service. Lived in County since 1826. Married 1847.	15
Mrs. Elizabeth Whitman	W. J. Whitman	D	24 SC	Entered service Apr 1862. Shot dead in battle Jackson, Mississippi 14 May 1864. Lived in County since 1878. Married 1861.	17
Mrs. Mary A. Lewis	D. B. Lewis	C	16 Ga	Entered service Jul 1861. Died Oct 1863 at Chattanooga, Tennessee from pneumonia. Lived in County since 1812. Married 1834. [large X placed over entire entry]	17
Mrs. Lottie E. Coker	John W. Coker		9 Ga Battalion	Entered service May 1862. Died Aug 1862 from measles and fever contracted in service. Lived in County since 1839. Married 1856. Transferred Fulton.	19
Mrs. Mary Whitaker	W. W. Whitaker	F	19 Ga	Entered service Mar 1863. Contracted sickness	19

Widow	Husband	Co	Regiment	Remarks	Page
				& died Nov 1863. Lived in County since 1837. Married 1857.	
Mrs. Nancy T. House	B. A. House	I	66 Ga	Entered service 1863. Died on diarrhea 1864. Lived in County since 1824. Married 1844.	21
Mrs. Mary E. Smith	John A. Smith	H	38 Ga	Entered service 1861. Killed battle Fisher's Hill, Virginia Aug 1864. Lived in County since 1830. Married 1855 or 1856.	21
Mrs. Sarah F. Oglesby	Thos. Oglesby	G	37 Ga	Entered service Mar 1862. Contracted sickness and died 15 Jun 1862. Lived in County since 1837. Married 1856.	23
Mrs. E. C. Burden	Woodson Burden	G	37 Ga	Entered service Mar 1862. died 7 Dec 1863 from sickness contracted in service. Lived in County since 1821. Married 1841.	23
Mrs. E. L. Graham	Elijah Graham	H	34 Ga	Entered service Mar 1862. Shot battle Jonesboro, Georgia 31 Aug 1864 and died in few days.	25

11

Widow	Husband	Co	Regiment	Remarks	Page
				Lived in County 10 Apr 1828. Married 1861.	
Mrs. Mary A. Greenaway	L. A. Greenaway	F	38 Ga	Entered service 1862. Died Jan 1863 Richmond, Virginia from sickness contracted in service. Lived in County since 1834. Married 1837.	25
Mars. Mary B. F. Teasley	James R. Teasley	H	Toombs' Legion	Entered service 1863. Died 10 Dec 1863 of fever contracted in service. Lived in County since 25 Aug 1830. Married 1845.	27
Mrs. Susan E. Lovinggood	Alfred H. Lovinggood	D	7 Ga Cavalry	Entered service Aug 1862. Shot and killed battle Trevilian Station, Virginia 11 Jun 1864. Lived in County since 1829. Married 1849.	27
Mrs. E. C. Taylor	J. J. Taylor	F	15 Ga	Entered service mar 1862. Contracted measles and died April 1862. Lived in County since 1826. Married 1857.	29
Mrs. Moriah Powell	Wiley Powell	F	38 Ga	Entered service 1862. Contracted sickness and died Fall 1863.	29

Widow	Husband	Co	Regiment	Remarks	Page
				Lived in County since 1840. Married 1846.	
Mrs. Mary E. Hall	Lindsey Hall	H	38 Ga	Entered service Aug 1862. Died of measles 15 Apr 1863. Lived in County since 1836. Married 1853.	31
Mrs. Sarah F. Parham	John W. Parham	H	38 Ga	Entered service Mar 1862. Shot dead battle Manassas, Virginia 1862. Lived in County since 1838. Married 1859.	31
Mrs. F. W. Hinton	Daniel C. Hinton	B	24 Ga	Entered service Aug 1861. Shot dead on battlefield 1864. Lived in County since 1834. Married 1857. [faint] to B. D. Hinton (son) 17 Feb 1899.	33
Mrs. S. B. Fortson	Jesse W. Fortson	F	38 Ga	Entered service May 1862. Died of fever Jul 1862 at Staunton, Virginia. Lived in County since 1838. Married 1858.	33
Mrs. Martha P. Colvard	Thos. Colvard	G	37 Ga	Entered service early 1864. Contracted sickness and died Fall 1864. Lived in County	35

Widow	Husband	Co	Regiment	Remarks	Page
				since Sep 1834. Married 1851.	
Mrs. Mary W. Scoggins	Jno. J. Scoggins	K	6 Ga	Entered service Jun 1861. Died in service Sep 1862 of chronic diarrhea. Lived in County since 1844. Married 1839.	35
Mrs. Frances P. Gaines	John R. Gaines	B	24 Ga	Entered service Aug 1861. Died of sickness Winter 1863. Lived in County since 1830. Married 1851.	37
Mrs. Mary E. Eavans	William Eavans	G	37 Ga	Entered service 1861. Served up to 1865. Shot dead battle Nashville, Tennessee. Lived in County since 1843. Married 1856. Delivered to son Jno. Evans 17 Feb 1899.	37
Mrs. Sarah Haynes	B. F. Haynes	D	9 Ga	Entered service Sep 1863. Died of fever 12 Dec 1863. Lived in County since 18 Feb 1828. Married 1846.	39
Mrs. Frances E. Partain	B. E. Partain	F	38 Ga	Entered service May 1861. Died 5 Feb 1864 of small pox at Guinea Station, Virginia. Lived in County since 1826.	39

14

Widow	Husband	Co	Regiment	Remarks	Page
				Married 1854.	
Mrs. Almeta S. Snider		B	1 Ga Reserves	Entered service Mar 1862. Wounded, sent to hospital, and contracted small pox. from which he died Oct. 1862. Lived in County since 1842. Married 1861.	41
Mrs. Susan Patton	T. J. Patton A. D. Patton	D	16 Ga	Contracted sickness from which he died Dec 1861 or Jan 1862. Lived in County since about 1826. Married 1840.	41
Mrs. Zilla A. Patton	A. D. Patton		Echols' Artillery	Entered service 1862 and served through war. Died from sickness contracted in service 1863. Widow born 1835. Married 1851. Delivered to John Wesley Patton 17 Feb 1899. Transferred.	41
Mrs. Mary A. E. Bowers	E. M. Bowers	A	19 Ga	Entered service Jun 1861. Contracted fever in service and died 6 or 7 May 1862. Lived in State since 1837. Married 1851.	43
Mrs. M. E.	Jeremiah	D	16 Ga	Entered service Jun 1862. Contracted	43

15

Widow	Husband	Co	Regiment	Remarks	Page
Thompson	Thompson			sickness from which he died Oct 1862. Lived in County since 12 Mar 1841.	
Mrs. Millie Powell	A. J. Powell	D	37 Ga	Entered service Mar 1862. Served until surrender. Contracted sickness from which he died Jan 1879. Lived in State since 1841. Born 12 Apr. Married 1859. Transferred Wilkes.	45
Mrs. Mary J. Jordan	F. M. Jordan	F	38 Ga	Entered service Jul 1862. Died 22 Nov 1869. Lived in State since 1833. Married Nov 1852. Delivered to J. A. Ginn 17 Feb 1899.	45
N. A. Jones	Nathan Jones	G	37 Ga	Entered service Mar 1862. Served 16 months. Died 1897. Married 1861. Transferred Wilkes 1904.	45
N. J. Greenway	T. J. Greenway	H	37 Ga	Served through war. Died 28 Feb 1895. Lived in State 71 years. Married 18 Dec 1851.	46
Mrs. L. Imry	J. C. Imry	F	38 Ga	Entered service Dec 1862. Served	46

Widow	Husband	Co	Regiment	Remarks	Page
				through war. Died 1892.. Lived in State since born 1837. Married Dec 1860.	
Mrs. S. E. Wheeler	D. M. Wheeler			Entered service Mar 1862. Served to Apr 1865. Shot at Manassas. Died Mar 1902. Married 1847.	46
M. A. Saxon	Abr Saxon	E	6 SC	Entered service 1852. Served to end of war. Died 1867.	46
Mrs. Mary F. Ginn	Thos. P. Ginn	H	Toombs' State Troops	Entered service 1863. Received hurt in service, that caused amputation of right leg, which finally killed him 1889. Lived in State 1841. Married 1857.	47
Mrs. A. A. Maxwell	W. H. Maxwell	F	38 Ga	Entered service Mar 1862. Contracted sickness in service and died Jun 1864. Chronic diarrhea. Lived in State since 28 June 1840. Married 1858.	47
E. J. Rousey	Arch Rousey	H	38 Ga	Served to surrender. Died 1881. Married 1852.	47
Mrs. Mary	James Johnson	A	1 Ga State	Entered service May 1864. Died 9	48

Widow	Husband	Co	Regiment	Remarks	Page
Johnson			Troops	Jan 1865 at Louisville, Kentucky, a prisoner of war. Lived in State since 17 Sep 1818. Married 1839. Transferred to Madison County.	
Mrs. Avey Mewborn	Wm A. Mewborn	G	37 Ga	Entered service Apr 1864. Contracted disease and died 9 Oct 1873. Lived in County since 1826. Married 1824.	48
J. T. Nash				~~Entered service Mar 1862 and served to surrender. Widow born 14 Mar 1825.~~	48
Mrs. Nettie McDonald	W. W. McDonald	H	34 Ga	Entered service 12 May 1862 and served to surrender. Died 5 Jun 1891. Lived in State since 1852. Married 1862.	48
Mrs. A. O. Jackson	Major J. M. Jackson		34 Ga	Entered service Jan 1862. Killed 31 Aug 1864 at Jonesboro, Georgia. Lived in State since 1831. Married 1851. Transferred.	49
Mrs. L. C. Harris	D. E. Harris	C	9 Ga Battalion	Entered service 1862. Died 9 Jul 1862 of typhoid fever.	49

18

Widow	Husband	Co	Regiment	Remarks	Page
				Lived in County since 20 Dec 1831. Married Jun 1853.	
Mrs. E. A. Adams	Thos. J. Adams	H	38 Ga	Entered service 1861 and served to surrender. Died immediately. Lived in County since Feb 1824. Married 1841.	49
Mrs. Mary A. Rousey	Edward Rousey	G	37 Ga	Entered service Mar 1862. Served to 1865. Married 25 Dec 1849.	49
Mrs. P. A. Anderson	W. A. Anderson	H	38 Ga	Entered service 1861 and served to surrender, 4 years. Lived in State since 1856. Married 15 Dec 1857.	50
Mrs. M. F. Alexander	T. R. Alexander	H	Toombs' State Troops	Entered service July 1864 and served to April 1865. T. R. A. 22 Mar 1883. Married 1855.	50
Mrs. S. R. Ginn	W. P. Ginn	K	2 Ga Militia	Entered service Feb 1863. Served 2 years. Widow born 5 Jan 1832. WP 1900 Au. Husband Pinkey Married 1848.	50
Mrs. N. S. Brown	Thos. J. Brown	G	37 Ga	Entered service 1863 and served through the war.	50

Widow	Husband	Co	Regiment	Remarks	Page
				Died 27 Sep 1887. Widow born 8 May 1837. Married 1858.	
P. R. Moats	W. A. Motes	F	38 Ga	Entered service Oct 1862. Served to 9 Apr 1865. Died 1897. Lived in State since 22 Mar 1842.	50
Caroline Hollmes	J. W. Holmes	F	Draft SC	Entered service Jun 1861 and served through the war. Died 21 Oct 1875. Lived 25 years. Married 1856.	51
E. M. Smith	J. J. Smith	F	Orr's Rifles SC Inf	Entered service 1861 and served to surrender. Died 15 Feb 1901. Lived in State 7 years. Married 1854.	51
Mrs. C. C. Green	W. A. Green, Surgeon		Cutt's Artillery	Entered service 1861 and served to 9 Apr 1865. Lived in State since 1834. Married 1854.	51
M. A. Maxwell	Geo. M. Maxwell	G	Wilkes Guards	Entered service Jun 1861 and served to May 1865. Married 1845.151	51
Mrs. Sallie Thomason	H. H. Thomason	K	2 Ga State Troops	Entered service 1862 and served to 1863. Married 1847. 17 Dec 1886.	51

Widow	Husband	Co	Regiment	Remarks	Page
	E. J. Mann	H	38 Ga	Entered service 1861 and served to the end of war. 5 May 1864 Wilderness. Widow born 15 Oct 1823	52
Mrs. Sarah Adams	James Adams	H	38 Ga	Served to surrender. Died 1886 of consumption. Married 1856.	52
Mrs. Elizabeth Kelley	James Kelley	G	37 Ga	Served 9 months. Died 1868 of consumption. Married 1856. 1822.	52
S. M. Scarborough	C. W. Scarborough	C	37 Ga	1836. Served 18 months to Nov 1863. Died 24 Dec 1888. Married 1851. Transferred Hall.	52
Mrs. Nettie McDonald	W. W. McDonald	H	34 Ga	Entered service 12 May 1862. 1891. Born 15 May 1844. Married 1862.	52
Mrs. Jane Balchin	Thomas Balchin	F	15 Ga	Entered service 15 Jul 1861 and served to Jun 1862. Died 15 Jun 1892. Born 1842. Married 1856.	52
Mrs. E. A. Adams	T. J. Adams	E	38 Ga	Entered service 1861 and served to surrender. 3 Nov 1868. Married 1842.	52

21

Widow	Husband	Co	Regiment	Remarks	Page
	A. Y. Gulley	H	38 Ga	Entered service 1861 and served 4 years.. Shot at Spotsylvania, Virginia. Old and infirm.	53
	G. W. Lovingood	C	15 Ga	Entered service 15 Jul 1861 and served to close of war. Born 1837.	53
	Thos. S. Davis	C	7 Ga Cavalry	25 Nov 1821. Entered service 1862 and served 2 years.	53
	J. M. Craft	I	2 Ky Battalion Cavalry	Born 1825. Served 14 months.	53
	G. W. Ginn	H	38 Ga	Born 1841. Entered service 1861. Wounded in left arm 12 May 1864 at Spotsylvania, Virginia.	53
	E. B. Higginbottham	F	38 Ga	Born 16 Dec 1838. Entered service 1862. Lost both legs 12 May 1862.	54
	W. H. Bond	H	15 Ga	Born 18 Jan 1838. Served 4 years.	54
	W. E. Fortson	I	15 Ga	Born 8 Sep 1833. Entered service 15 Jul 1861 and served to 9 Apr 1865.	54
	F. O. Bailey	F	15 Ga	Born 1841. Entered service 15 Jul 1861 and served	54

Widow	Husband	Co	Regiment	Remarks	Page
				to 9 Apr 1865. Shot through right arm, disabling since 2nd Manassas.	
J. W. Christian					54
Mrs. Nancy A. Jones	Nathan Jones	G	37 Ga	Served 2 years. transferred Wilkes.	54
	J. H. W. Colquitt	K	3 Ga State Troops	Born 23 Jan 1838. Entered service 1862.	55
	E. M. Roberts	C	15 Ga	Born 4 Mar 1824. Entered service Jul 1861.	55
	John Terry	F	15 Ga	Born 1822. Entered service Mar 1862.	55
	A. C. Hendricks	G	37 Ga	Born 16 Dec 1834. Served 3 years. Transferred.	55
	Fran Smith	F	15 Ga	Born 17 Oct 1828. Entered service Jul 1861 and served to 9 Apr 1865.	55
Mrs. Purnia Lyttle	Absalom Lyttle	F	50 Ga	Transferred from Franklin. Married 1852. Died 28 May 1888.	56
Mrs. S. E. Wheelis	D. M. Wheelis	C	15 Ga	Entered service July 1861. Married 1847. Died 1902.	56
Henrietta Faulkner	C. W. Faulkner		Roswell Battalion Cavalry	Served 10 months. Married 1863. Died 1903. Transferred to	56

23

Widow	Husband	Co	Regiment	Remarks	Page
				Griffin, Georgia.	
Rachel Christian	Will Christian	H	38 Ga	Entered service 1862 and served to Summer 1865. Married 1852.	56
Mrs. R. C. Mattox	W. H. Mattox	I	15 Ga	Entered service 15 Jul 1861. Married 1858.	56
Mrs. Emily C. Davis	T. S. Davis	C	7 Ga Cavalry	Indigent List before death. Married 1845.	56
Mrs. F. J. Fagan	L. M. Fagan	A	24 Ga	At time of death on Indigent List. Married 1849.	56
Mrs. Mary E. Busby	W. Y. Busby	I	44 Ga	On Indigent List at time of death.	56
Mrs. Mary E. Haley	Willis Haley	K	2 SC Rifles	Served 6 months.	56
	J. W. Bond	H	38 Ga	Born 20 Dec 1830. Served 4 years.	57
	J. T. Nash	G	37 Ga	Born 14 Mar 1825. Served 3 years. Dead 19 Sep 1904.	57
	J. M. Broadwell	F	15 Ga	Born 28 Jan 1823. Entered service Jul 1861 and served to end of war.	57
	M. M. Symon	I	15 Ga	Born 27 May 1834. Served 3 years.	57
	B. T. Brown	F	38 Ga	Born 1841. Shot through left shoulder 13 Dec 1862 Fredericksburg,	57

24

Widow	Husband	Co	Regiment	Remarks	Page
				Virginia.	
Mrs. S. E. Clark	H. H. Clark	C	7 Ga Cavalry	Served 3 years. Married 1851. Died 15 Dec 1905.	58
	T. N. Wausley	F	38 ga	Born 15 Oct 1833. Served 2½ years.	59
	J. C. Young	A	4 Ga Militia	Born 10 May 1834. Served 3 years.	59
	Jas. C. Harper	H	Toombs' State Troops	Born 11 Dec 1821. Served 2½ years.	59
	W. T. Ginn	K	2 Ga	Born 12 Jan 1827. Served 2 years.	59
	W. Y. Bussey	I	44 Ga	Born 18 Mar 1826. Served 3 years.	59
	A. E. Hammond	G	37 Ga	Entered service Mar 1862 and served to 22 Jul 1864, when shot.	59
	J. Herring	B	24 Ga	Born 10 Jun 1823. Served 4 years.	61
	H. W. Bond	H	Toombs' State Troops	Born 1807. Served 7 months.	61
	J. F. Butler	C	7 Ga Cavalry	Born 2 Jun 1824. Served 3 years.	61
	S. J. Nash	A	1 Ga State Troops	Born 1 Mar 1818. Served 10 months.	61
	Thos. Phelps	A	1 Ga State Troops	Born 1816. Served 8 months.	61
	W. J. Simmonds	A	37 Ga	Born 1842. Lost right leg below knee 31 Nov 1864 at battle of Franklin,	62

Widow	Husband	Co	Regiment	Remarks	Page
				Tennessee. Transferred.	
	J. E. Campbell	H	38 Ga	Born 23 Apr 1842. Entered service 6 Mar 1862 and served to surrender 9 Apr 1865. Wounded 1 Jun 1864 2nd Cold Harbor, Virginia.	62
	Charley Dickerson	I	15 Ga	Born 4 Mar 1834. Entered service mar 1862 and served 3 years.	62
	Sam Dixon	C	7 Ga Cavalry	Born 1847. Entered service 1863 and served to Apr 1865.	62
	R. H. Kidd	E	38 Ga	Born 1833. Entered service May 1862 and served to surrender 9 Apr 1865. Transferred Madison.	62
	W. T. Scott	D	7 Ga Cavalry	Born 15 Jun 1826. Served 18 months.	63
	J. F. Wise	A	Gardens Battery	Born 13 Oct 1828. Served 15 months.	63
	~~W. T. Scott~~	~~D~~	~~7 Ga Cavalry~~	~~Born 15 Jun 1826. Served 18 months.~~	63
	J. F. Wise	A	Gardens Battery	Born 4 Mar 1826. Served 15 months.	63
	A. W. Dixon	A	7 Ga Cavalry	Born 30 Jun 1831. Served 3 years.	63

Widow	Husband	Co	Regiment	Remarks	Page
	T. M. Hill	I	18 Ga	Born 1835. Entered service 1861 and served to surrender.	64
	J. N. Burriss	H	52 Ga	Born 1 Nov 1830. Entered service 1863 and served 8 months. Discharged disability.	64
	M. V. Bagwell	C	16 Ga	Born 1846. Entered service 1863 and served to surrender.	64
	D. M. Dabbs	I	8 Ga	Born 22 1841. Served 4 years to surrender. Transferred Fulton County 1904.	64
	Sam Hall	I	14 SC	Born 3 Sep 1825. Served 18 months.	65
	J. M. Bradford	A	7 Ga	Born 27 Apr. Served 3 years.	65
	A. A. James	I	15 Ga	Born 25 Feb 1834. Entered service 15 Jul and served to surrender.	65
	W. T. Frost	C	16 Ga	Born 19 Feb 1839. Entered service Feb 1862 and served 3 years to end of war.	65
	R. C. Nash	H	Toombs' State Troops	Born 1826. Entered service 1863 and served 18 months.	65

Widow	Husband	Co	Regiment	Remarks	Page
	J. M. Moon	C	15 Ga	Born 19 Nov 1834. Entered service 15 Jul 1861 and served to close of war.	65
	W. G. Moon	H	38 Ga	Born 1843. Entered service Mar 1863 and served to surrender, 3 years. Thus he is badly impaired.	66
	W. J. Dudley	E	37 Ga	Born 1831. Entered service May 1862 and served to 19 Sep 1863.	66
	L. W. Saxon	D	10 Ga	Born 1826. Entered service Apr 1863. Wounded 6 Apr 1865 in right leg and arm. Bryant's Brigade.	66
	Marshall Hill	I	14 SC	Born 1833. Enlisted Sep 1861 and served to 1 Jul 1863. Lost left leg above knee at battle Gettysburg, Pennsylvania. McGowan's Brigade.	66
	R. L. Daniel	K	2 Ga State Troops	Born 7 Jun 1844. Entered service Oct 1861 and served 2½ years.	67
	W. H. Carpenter	A	2 Ky Battalion	Born 1836. Served 2¼ years.	67
	Jas. W. Smith	A	1 Ga State	Born 30 Nov 1839. Entered service	67

Widow	Husband	Co	Regiment	Remarks	Page
			Troops	1863 and served 2 years. South Carolina Nov 1864.	
	A. M. Sumate	E	7 SC	Born 15 Apr 1840. Entered service Jan 1861 and served 28 months. Discharged Aug 1863 disability.	67
	J. D. Holms	F	15 Ga	Born 26 Aug 1837. Entered service 15 Jul 1861 and served to 9 Apr 1865.	67
	W. E. Fortson	F	15 Ga	Born Sep 1832. Entered service 15 Jul 1861 and served to surrender 9 Apr 1865.	67
	Jesse Willis	H	37 Ga	Born Jan 1840. Served 3 years.	68
	J. B. Terry	K	2 Ga State Troops	Born 1826. Enlisted 162 and served to 1865.	68
	H. C. Belker	A	1 SC	Born 1840. Served 4½ years.	68
	W. G. Sanders	A	1 Ga State Troops	Born 1845. Entered service Mar 1864 and served to surrender. Smith's Brigade.	68
	S. D. Colden			Born 1830. Entered service Mar 1862, served 8 months, and discharged for disability.	68

Widow	Husband	Co	Regiment	Remarks	Page
	W. H. Christian	H	Dunn's Regiment	Born 1837. Entered service 1 Oct 1864 and served to 9 Apr 1865.	68
	J. H. Jones	I	15 Ga	Born 25 Dec 1838. Served to 9 Apr 1865.	69
	J. W. Eavenson	F	38 Ga	Born 28 May 1841. Entered service 1861 and served to 1864.	69
	E. N. Kinnebrew	C	15 Ga	Born 1842. Entered service 15 Jul 1861 and served to 9 Apr 1865.	69
	E. M. Bond	H	38 Ga	Born 28 Feb 1838. Entered service Oct 1861 and served to 1864. 2nd Manassas, Virginia 31 Aug 1862.	69
	J. T. Shaw	E	Lumpkin's Artillery	Born 1829. Served 1½ years.	69
	A. C. Hendricks	G	37	Born 2 Dec 1834. Entered service Mar 1862 and served to 9 Apr 1865.	69
	J. E. Anderson	F	Holcomb Legion	Born 1837. Served to 1863. Lost left leg above knee, 2nd Manassas, 31 Aug 1862.	69
	N. L. Bailey	G	37 Ga	Born 29 Apr 1832. Entered service Mar 1862 and	70

Widow	Husband	Co	Regiment	Remarks	Page
				served to surrender of Johnson's Army, May 1865.	
	J. W. Booth	H	38 Ga	Born 1836. Entered service Mar 1862. Lost left leg Fishers Hill, Virginia 24 Sep 1864.	70
	Henry Dunn	C	16 Ga	Born 25 Jan 1832. Entered service 1861 and served to 9 Apr 1865.	70
	W. C. Simmons	A	16 Ga	Born 1835. Entered service Jul 1861 and served to 9 Apr 1865.	70
	M. H. Scogins	D	41 Ga	Born 1823. Served 3 years.	70
	W. C. Cox	I	16 Ga	Born 1840. Served 4 years.	70
	J. Allen Maxwell	H	Toombs' State Troops	Born 1823. Served 8 months.	71
	T. S. Grimes	I	15 Ga	Born 13 Aug 1836. Entered service 15 Jul 1862 and served to 17 Sep 1862. Shot through right shoulder and leg bust. Sharpsburg, Maryland.	71
	G. W. Ginn	H	38 Ga	Born 1841. Shot battle Spotsylvania 12 May 1864.	71
	J. L. Wilhite	H	37 Ga	Born 12 Nov 1830. Served to battle	71

31

Widow	Husband	Co	Regiment	Remarks	Page
				Missionary Ridge 12 Nov 1863. Shot through left arm, disabling same.	
	D. M. Whelis	C	15 Ga	Born 1830. Served through war.	71
	J. M. Craft	A	2 Ky Cavalry	Born 1826. Served 3 years.	71
	William Pulliam	H	38 Ga	Born 18 Jul 1831. Shot through right shoulder 27 Aug 1862, disabling same.	72
	William Oglesby	H	38 Ga	Born 1827. Wounded 13 Dec 1862 Fredericksburg, Virginia. Shot through right shoulder, disabling same. Gordon's Brigade.	72
	J. N. Colvard	H	38 Ga	Born 1841. Battle Cold Harbor, Virginia 27 Jun 1862. Lost middle finger on right hand.	72
	S. J. Anderson	H	12 Ky Cavalry	Born 10 Sep 1842. Entered service Sep 1863 and served to end of war.	72
	C. F. Christian	H	38 Ga	Born 1844. Served 2 years. Gordon's Brigade. Fishers Hill Sep 1864.	72

Widow	Husband	Co	Regiment	Remarks	Page
	T. T. Owens	A	15 Ga	Born 1 Jan 1836. Entered service 15 Jul 1861 and served to surrender.	73
	T. A. Moore	H	38 Ga	Born 1834. Entered service 1861 and served 4 years.	73
	T. F. Rowzee	F	15 Ga	Born 30 Jul 1837. Entered service 15 July 1861 and served to Lee's surrender.	73
	R. B. Galloway	F	15 Ga	Born 1835. Entered service 15 Jul 1861 and served 4 years to Lee's surrender.	73
	F. E. Owens	A	15 Ga	Born 1838. Entered service Mar 1862 and served to Lee's surrender.	73
	J. J. Burden	G	37 Ga	Born 3 Dec 1833. Entered service Jun 1862 and served 3 years.	73
	W. H. Brough	G	14 SC	Born 1 May 1838. Entered service Apr 1861 and served to April 1865.	74
	W. P. Davis	C	2 SC	Born 11 Sep 1837. Entered service Nov 1861 and served 3½ years.	74
	J. M. Cosby	C	7 Ga	Born 27 Aug 1845. Entered service	74

33

Widow	Husband	Co	Regiment	Remarks	Page
			Cavalry	Nov 1862 and served to close of war.	
	R. M. Heard	C	7 Ga Cavalry	Born 7 Apr 1836. Entered service Aug 1862 and served to Lee's surrender. Wounded 29 Oct 1864.	74
	C. W. Maxwell	H	38 Cav	Born 7 Feb 1845. Entered service 1862 and served to 1863.	74
	S. J. W. Hunt	F	38 Ga	Born 28 Jun 1838. Entered service 1862 and served to 1865.	74
	J. D. Caswell	G	37 Ga	Born 12 Jan 1846. Entered service May 1863 and served to Apr 1864.	75
	J. C. Thornton	F	38 Ga	Born 8 Aug 1844. Entered service Feb in 1861. 13 Dec 1862. served to Lee's surrender.	75
	T. R. White	I	15 Ga	Entered service 15 July 1861 and served to surrender 9 Apr 1865.	75
	G. W. Hall	H	38 Ga	Born 10 Feb 1834. Entered service 1862 and served to Dec 1864. Discharged disability.	75

Widow	Husband	Co	Regiment	Remarks	Page
	A. W. Vaughn	C	15 Ga	Born 8 Nov 1826. Entered service 15 Jul. Shot through hip 1 Jul 1863. Battle Gettysburg, Pennsylvania. In Asylum.	75
	G. S. Bell	C	15 Ga	Born 25 Jul 1835. Entered service Mar 1862. Served 10 months. Substitute.	75
	J. H. Higginbotham	K	4 Ga Reserves	Born 1840. Entered service 1864 and served 1 year. Transferred Hart.	76
	L. L. Clark	F	15 Ga	80 years old. Entered service 15 Jul 1861 and served 8 months.	76
	W. C. Dennane	K	1 Ga State Troops	Born Feb 1836. Served 11 months. Transferred Hart.	76
	C. W. Falker		Roswell Battalion Cavalry	Born 1832. Entered service 1864 and served 10 months. Transferred Spaulding.	76
	W. G. Field	F	22 SC	Born 1835. Entered service Jan 1862 and served 3 years. 3 Nov 1893.	76
	J. W. Ballard	C	7 Ga Cavalry	Born 1835. Entered service 1862 and served to	76

Widow	Husband	Co	Regiment	Remarks	Page
				9 Apt 1865. Transferred Lincoln County.	
	L. M. Adams	H	2 Ga State Troops	Born 1837. Entered service 1863 and served 2 years.	76
	T. B. Wells	C	15 Ga	Born 1841. Entered service 15 Jul 1861 and served to surrender.	77
	J. H. Cox	H	2 Ga State Troops	Born 1822. Entered service 1864 and served 9 months.	77
	T. B. Smith	C	15 Ga	Born 1835. Entered service 1862 and served to surrender.	77
	D. H. Warren	H	Toombs' State Troops	Born 1839. Entered service 1863 and served 6 months.	77
	W. A. Craft	F	15 Ga	Born 1840. Entered service March 1862 and served to 9 Apr 1865.	77
	Willis Bryant	H	Toombs' State Troops	85 years. Served 12 months.	77
	A. L. White	F	15 Ga	Born 1840. Served to surrender.	77
	T. J. Ginn	K	2 Ga State Troops	Born 1825. Entered service Feb 1863 and served 2	78

Widow	Husband	Co	Regiment	Remarks	Page
				years. 31 Aug 1864	
	H. F. Hamilton	E	16 Ga Battalion	Born 1847. Entered service Jan 1864. Organic trouble, chilblains. Transferred from Jackson.	78
	L. G. [faint]	C	Toombs' State Troops	Born 15 Feb 1832. Served 16 months. Transferred Oglethorpe.	78
	D. S. Kerlin	C	15 Ga	Born 1834. Entered service 15 Jul 1861 and served to Lee's surrender.	78
	A. J. Andrew	A	15 Ga	Born 1836. Entered service Mar 1862 and served 3 years.	78
	W. L. Lovinggood	C	15 Ga	Born 7 Jul 1834. Entered service Mar 1862 and served 3 years to surrender.	78
	J. F. Stilwell	C	14 Ga	Born 25 June 1835. Entered service Jun 1861 and served to surrender.	79
	H. J. Cofer	C	Toombs' State Troops	Born 10 May 1845. Entered service May 1864 and served to Lee's surrender.	79
	W. H. Clark	C	7 Ga Cavalry	Born 1823. Entered service 1863 and served to	79

Widow	Husband	Co	Regiment	Remarks	Page
				surrender.	
	J. W. Turner	G	37 Ga	Born 1823. Served to Johnson's surrender.	79
	J. W. Ouzts	K	14 SC	Born 1834. Entered service Aug 1861 and served to surrender.	79
	M. J. Thornton	I	15 Ga	Born 1840. Entered service 15 Jul 1861 and served to surrender.	79
	B. T. Ingram	A	59 Ga	Wounded 1 Jul 1863 in Pennsylvania. Shot through hip.	79
	G. B. Rhodes	A	15 Ga	Born 1838.	80
	E. V. Clark	G	22 SC	Born 1835. Entered service Jan 1862 and served 2 years.	80
	B. P. Ingram	A	59 Ga	Born Aug 1833. Wounded 2 Jul 1863. Anderson's Brigade.	80
	Jno. W. Brownlee			Born 31 May 1830. Entered service at Elberton, Georgia and served 24 months. Braumgard's Battery.	80
	W. B. Chapman		Corput's Battery	Born Mar 1833. Entered service Feb 1862 at Rome, Georgia and served	80

Widow	Husband	Co	Regiment	Remarks	Page
				to surrender. .	
	W. G. Anderson			Born 1838. Entered service 15 July 1861 and served to 9 Apr 1865.	80
	J. J. Manning	F	24 SC	Born 1838. Served 4 years.	80
	W. G. Anderson	I	15 Ga	Born 1838. Entered service 15 July 1861 and served to surrender.	81
	W. H. Snellings	C	7 Ga Cavalry	Born 1843. Served to end of war.	81
	J. M. Halley	G	Butler's SC Regiment	Born 1842. Entered service Spring 1863 and served to Apr 1865.	81
	L. M. Fagan	A	24 Ga	Born 1838. Served 4 years to Apr 1865.	81
	C. L. Berger	C	44 Ga	Born 1842. Entered service 1862 and served to surrender. Wounded Chancellorsville, Virginia. Shot through right shoulder 2 May. Invalid. Transferred Clarke County.	81
	W. B. Chapman		Corput's Artillery	Served 3 years. Discharged 9 Apr 1865. 72 years old.	81

Widow	Husband	Co	Regiment	Remarks	Page
	D. B. Alexander	F	15 Ga	Born Feb 1841. Served 4 years.	81
	W. E. Thornton	H	Toombs' State Troops	Entered service Jul 1864 and served to Mar 1865.	82
	J. M. Brown	C	7 Ga Cavalry	Served 3 years.	82
	T. D. Biggs	I	15 Ga	Entered service 15 July 1861.	82
	J. M. Brown	H	38 Ga	Born 1834. Entered service Mar 1864 and served to surrender of Lee's Army.	82
	J. W. Christian	H	38 Ga	Entered service Sep 1861. Disabled Sharpsburg, Maryland.	82
	D. C. Cosby	C	15 Ga	Entered service 15 Jul 1861 and served to 9 Apr 1865.	82
	C. J. Lovinggood	C	15 Ga	Entered service 15 Jul 1861 and served to 9 Apr 1865.	82
	Abda Oglesby	H	38 Ga	Entered service 1861 and served to Spotsylvania, Virginia.	82
	J. F. Powell	E	Ga Reserves	Entered service Jun 1864 and served to 26 May 1865.	82
	G. W. Snellings	C	15 Ga	Born 1841. Entered service 1861 and served to 9 Apr 1865.	83

Widow	Husband	Co	Regiment	Remarks	Page
	G. T. Snellings	C	7 Ga Cavalry	Enlisted 1862. 60 years.	83
	J. S. Tate	C	15 Ga	Entered service Jul 1861 and served to 9 Apr 1865.	83
	M. E. Fortson	I	15 Ga	Born 18 Mar 1840. Entered service Jul 1861 and served to 9 Apr 1865.	83
	L. L. Baily	G	37 Ga	Entered service May 1862 and served to 26 Apr 1865.	83
	S. B. Guest	G	2 SC Rifles	Entered service Jun 1862. Surrendered at Appomattox, Virginia 9 Apr 1865.	83
	J. W. Scoggins		Echols' Artillery	Entered service 1862. 65 years.	83
	J. H. Higginbotham	K	4 Ga Reserves	Transferred Hart County.	83
	V. E. Harper		7 Ga Cavalry	Born 1835. Transferred Screven County. Served 3 years.	83
	W. T. Smith	C	15 Ga		83
	~~Virgil E. Harper~~	~~C~~	~~7 Ga Cavalry~~	~~Served 3 years~~	83
	John W. Christian	H	38 Ga	Born 1836. Transferred from Invalid to Indigent. Entered service Sep and served to surrender.	84

Widow	Husband	Co	Regiment	Remarks	Page
	A. J. Webb	I	15 Ga	Served 4 years. Transferred from Clarke County. 67 years.	84
	J. W. Burden	D	11 Ga Cavalry	Born 1822. 84 years old. Paralysis. No property.	84
	~~J. H. Higginbotham~~	K	~~4 Ga Reserves~~	~~Transferred from Hart County Jan 1904.~~	84
	Abram Dixon	F	8 Ala	Transferred from Madison 6 Jan 1906. Served 4 years.	84
	W. M. McIntosh	B	1 Ga Reserves	Born Feb 1847. Enlisted Apr or Mar and served 13 months.	84
	J. H. Fleming	H	1 Ga Reserves	Entered service Jul 1864 and served to surrender.	84
	N. B. Cosby	C	15 Ky	Entered service Mar 1862 and served to surrendered.	84
	Joel W. Moore	A	1 Ga Reserves	Born 1821. Served 3 years.	85
	G. T. Snelling				85
	A. O. Hall	D	7 SC	Born 1840. Entered service 1861 and served 4 years.	85
	J. T. Ridgway			Enlisted Company G, Confederate	85

42

Widow	Husband	Co	Regiment	Remarks	Page
				Troops. Served to surrender.	
	Clark Mattox	I	15 Ga	Born 1838. Entered service 1861 and served to Sep 1862.	85
	J. D. Adams	I	15 Ga	Entered service 15 Jul 1861 and served to Appomattox, Virginia.	85
	J. C. Thornton	C	7 Ga Cavalry	Entered service 1863 and served to 1864.	85
	H. C. McEwen	D	16 Ga	Entered service 1863 and served to 1865.	85
	J. C. Chafin	E	38 Ga	Born 1847. Served to surrender. Transferred from Madison County 7 Jan 1907.	85
	S. A. McIntox	B		Enlisted 1862 and served to surrender.	86
	J. T. Ridgway	G	Durson's Command	Born 1844. Served 9 months.	86
	E. P. Bailey	G	37 Ga	Born 1838. Entered service Mar 1862 and served to surrender.	86
	T. J. Hester	I	15 Ga	Born 1840. Entered service Jul 1861 and served to surrender.	86

Roster of Company I, 15th Georgia Infantry

The typewritten, three-page roster appears to have been inserted into the back of the original volume at the end of the list of pensioners.

Roster of Co., "I" 15th. Ga. Inf.

Smith, Joseph T.	Captain	Dead
Shannon, P. J.	1st Lieut.	Dead
Clark, W. J.	2nd Lieut.	Dead
Mattox, William H., Jr	3rd Lieut.	Dead

Smith, Francis W.	1st Sergeant	Dead
Marcus, M. A.	2nd Sergeant	Dead
Hollingsworth, William J.	4th Sergeant	(unknown)

(The above man was from S. Carolina and his whereabouts and whether living or dead is unknown.)

Hester, T. J.	1st Corporal	Dead
Mattox, N. M.	2nd Corporal	Dead
Cleveland, R. W.	4th Corporal	30 W. Church St., Elberton, Ga.
Adams, A. G.	4th Corporal	Dead

PRIVATES

Adams, J. D.	Dead	Adams, Richard C.	Dead
Adams, W. H.	Dead	Alexander, G. L.	Dead (?)
Almond (or Almand) G. M.	Dead	Anderson, W. D.	Dead
Arnold, J. B. D.	Dead		
Biggs, T. D.	Dead	Bond, Francis K.	Dead
Bond, J. B.	Dead	Bond, Martin R.	Unknown
Brown, A. F.	Dead	Booth, J. C.	Dead
Brown, W. H.	Dead	Brown, S. W.	Dead
Buffington, R. T.	Dead	Bruce, J. A.	Dead
Butler, W. S.	Dead	Buffington, W. R.	Dead

Clark, W. T.	Dead	
Coker, B. P.	Unknown	
Cleveland, W. L.	Dead	

Dedwyler, J. L.	Dead	Dickerson, C. Y.	Unknown
Dickerson, J. E.	Unknown		

44

Faulker (or Falkner) I. N.	Dead	Ford, J. A.	Dead
Ford, Jordan R.	Unknown	Fortson, A. T.	Dead
Fortson, D. A.	Dead	Fortson, E. R.	Dead
Fortson, J. B.	Dead	Fortson, J. W. (or J. U.)	Dead
Fortson, M. E.	Dead	Fortson, W. W.	Dead
*Fraley, Lafayette (don't remember)		Franklin, A.	`Unknown
Franklin, H.	Dead		

Gaines, Francis	Dead	Gaines, J. A.	Dead
Gaines, L.	Unknown	Gaines, P. C.	#3, Elberton, Ga.
Gaines, T.	Dead	Gaulding, W. D.	unknown
		(last time heard of was at Carlton, Ga.)	

Hadden, (or Haddon) C. C. believe dead.		Hailey, G. W.	unknown Miss.
Hammond, W. H.	Dead	Harbin, J. M.	unknown Carolina
Higginbotham, E.	Dead	Hollingsworth, W. T.	unknown Carolina

James, A. A.	Dead	Jones, J. H.	Dead

King, J. M.	Unknown	King, Rufus	(Went West believe dead.)
King, W. B.	Unknown (believe dead)		

Loehr, G.	Dead	Lumpkin, S. J.	(Believe Dead)

Mailey, J. R.	Dead	Mailey, J. M.	Unknown
Mailey, M. V.	Dead	Marous, M. J. (pvt. & 2nd Corpl.) Dead	
Mason, A.	Dead		
Moon, W. P.	unknown	Moon, J. S.	Unknown
McClellan, T.	unknown		

Norman, E. B.	Dead		

Patterson, W. W. Believes lives in Hart Co.		Pearson, G. W.	unknown
Perryman, J. A.	Dead	Pledger, S. L.	Dead
Pledger, W. P.	Dead	Pulliam, J.	Dead
Pulliam, M. E.	Dead	Pulliam, N. B.	Dead

Roberts, W. H.	Dead		

45

Seymour, M.	Dead	*Smith, G. C.	unknown
Smith, H. G.	Dead	Smith, W. P.	Dead
Staedman, L.	Dead		
Taylor, J. H. C.	Dead	Taylor, J. J.	Dead
Teasley, A. J.	Dead	Tennent, H.	unknown (Carolina)
Tennent, O.	unknown (Carolina)	Tennent, W.	Dead
Thornton, M.	Dead	Treadwell, T.	Dead
Wansley, W. J.	Dead	Webb, A. J.	Dead
Webb, J. C.	unknown	Webb, M.	Dead
White, Tinsley R. (Soldier's Home)		Williams, G. T.	Dead
Williams, W. W.	Dead	Wood, R. A. (Don't remember}	

The above information was furnished through the courtesy of R. W. Cleveland, of 30 Church Street, Elberton, Ga., and a former member of Co. I, 15th Ga. He is now 84 years of age and enjoying fairly good health and a splendid memory.

All notations to the effect that soldier is unknown means that informant does not know of whereabouts or whether living or dead. All notations to the effect of #don't remember" means that informant has no recollection of this soldier whatsoever.

This July 19th, 1927.

_____

Ordinary Elbert County, Georgia

I have only two of the above number on my pension rolls, namely the above informant and P. C. Gaines.

Volume II

On the spine of the second original volume is the title *Pension Record*. The first page consists of printed instructions on how to keep the printed pension rolls. The instructions specify that the clerk should keep three separate lists, one each for widows, soldiers, and disabled soldiers. Unfortunately, the clerk did not follow the instructions, instead altering the printed columns, failing to record all of the information about each pensioner, and keeping nine separate lists. The first four lists include the soldiers pension rolls for the years 1929 through 1932. The next four lists include the widows pension rolls for the same years. The ninth list appears to be an overflow from the first two lists.

1929 Pension Roll

The following table presents the transcribed information in seven columns. The first column includes a consecutive number assigned to each pensioner, the second column is the name of the pensioner, the third column includes all of the nonpayment related information recorded by the clerk, and the last four columns include the pension amounts paid in each of the four quarters of 1929.

No.	Name	Remarks	1st Qtr	2nd Qtr	3rd Qtr	4th Qtr
1	Bailey, F. O.	Died 6 Jun 1929	$50			
2	Brown, S. G.		$50	$50	$50	$50
3	Burden, J. A.		$50	$50	$50	$50
4	Childs, J. B.		$50	$50	$50	$50
5	Childs, S. G.		$50	$50	$50	$50
6	Cleveland, R. W.		$50	$50	$50	$50
7	Conwell, J. D.		$50	$50	$50	$50
8	Eavenson, J. W.		$50	$50	$50	$50
9	Fleming, J. H.		$50	$50	$50	$50
10	Gaines, W. S.		$50	$50	$50	$50
11	Gulley, J. W.		$50	$50	$50	$50
12	Hamm, P. H.		$50	$50	$50	$50
13	Heard, E. B.		$50	$50	$50	$50
14	Hudson, W. A. C.	Died 6 Dec 1929	$50	$50	$50	$50
15	Jones, J. M.	Died 31 Jan 1930	$50	$50	$50	$50
16	Maxwell, C. W.		$50	$50	$50	$50
17	Oglesby, D. P.	Died 31 May 1929	$50			

No.	Name	Remarks	1st Qtr	2nd Qtr	3rd Qtr	4th Qtr
18	Snellings, G. W.		$50	$50	$50	$50
19	Swift, T. M.		$50	$50	$50	$50
20	Tate, W. E.	Died 30 Aug 1929	$50			
21	Thornton, J. W.		$50	$50	$50	$50
22	Willis, T. F.		$50	$50	$50	$50
23	Gaines, J. A.	Died 23 Aug 1929				
24	Booth, J. J.				$50	$50

1930 Pension Roll

The following table presents the transcribed information in seven columns. The first column includes a consecutive number assigned to each pensioner, the second column is the name of the pensioner, the third column includes all of the nonpayment related information recorded by the clerk, and the last four columns include the pension amounts paid in each of the four quarters of 1930.

No.	Name	Remarks	1st Qtr	2nd Qtr	3rd Qtr	4th Qtr
1	Brown, S. G.	Died 6 Nov 1930	$50	$50	$50	$50
2	Burden, J. A.		$50	$50	$50	$50
3	Childs, J. B.		$50	$50	$50	$50
4	Childs, S. G.		$50	$50	$50	$50
5	Cleveland, R. W.		$50	$50	$50	$50
6	Conwell, J. D.		$50	$50	$50	$50
7	Eavenson, J. W.		$50	$50	$50	$50
8	Fleming, J. H.		$50	$50	$50	$50
9	Gaines, W. S.		$50	$50	$50	$50
10	Gulley, J. W.	Placed in Soldiers Home 31 Mar 1930. Died 12 Jun 1930	$50			
11	Hamm, P. H.		$50	$50	$50	$50
12	Heard, E. B.		$50	$50	$50	$50
13	Jones, J. M.	Died 31 Jan 1930 Pension paid to Widow	$50	$50	$50	$50
14	Maxwell, C. W.		$50	$50	$50	$50
15	Snellings, G. W.		$50	$50	$50	$50

No.	Name	Remarks	1st Qtr	2nd Qtr	3rd Qtr	4th Qtr
16	Swift, T. M.		$50	$50	$50	$50
17	Thornton, J. W.		$50	$50	$50	$50
18	Willis, T. F.		$50	$50	$50	$50
19	Booth, J. J.		$50	$50	$50	$50
20	Vaughn, H. D.			$50	$50	$50

1931 Pension Roll

The following table presents the transcribed information in four columns. The first column includes a consecutive number assigned to each pensioner, the second column is the name of the pensioner, the third column includes all of the nonpayment related information recorded by the clerk, and the fourth column includes the pension amounts paid in each of the months of 1931.

No.	Name	Remarks	Months Paid
1	Burden, J. A.	Died 3 Apr 1931	$30 Jan - Feb
2	Childs, J. B.		$30 Jan - Dec
3	Childs, S. G.		$30 Jan - Dec
4	Cleveland, R. W.		$30 Jan - Dec
5	Conwell, J. D.		$30 Jan - Dec
6	Eavenson, J. W.		$30 Jan - Dec
7	Fleming, J. H.		$30 Jan - Dec
8	Gaines, W. S.		$30 Jan - Dec
9	Hamm, P. H.		$30 Jan - Dec
10	Heard, E. B.		$30 Jan - Dec
11	Maxwell, C. W.		$30 Jan - Dec
12	Snellings, G. W.	June Payment late	$30 Jan – May, $15 Jun, $30 Jul - Dec
13	Swift, T. M.	June Payment late	$30 Jan – May, $15 Jun, $30 Jul - Dec
14	Thornton, J. W.		$30 Jan - Dec
15	Booth, J. J.		$30 Jan - Dec
16	Vaughn, H. D.	Died 27 Oct 1931 Pd. Widow fol. Bal. yr.	$30 Jan - Dec

No.	Name	Remarks	Months Paid
17	Willis, T. F.	Died 10 Jan 1931	

1932 Pension Roll

The following table presents the transcribed information in four columns. The first column includes a consecutive number assigned to each pensioner, the second column is the name of the pensioner, the third column includes all of the nonpayment related information recorded by the clerk, and the fourth column includes the pension amounts paid in each of the months of 1932.

No.	Name	Remarks	Months Paid
1	Booth, J. J.		$30 Jan - Sep
2	Childs, J. B.		$30 Jan - Sep
3	Childs, S. G.		$30 Jan - Sep
4	Cleveland, R. W.		$30 Jan - Sep
5	Conwell, J. D.	Died 28 Sep 1832	$30 Jan - Aug
6	Eavenson, J. W.		$30 Jan - Sep
7	Fleming, J. H.		$30 Jan - Sep
8	Gaines, W. S.		$30 Jan - Sep
9	Hamm, P. H.		$30 Jan - Sep
10	Heard, E. B.		$30 Jan - Sep
11	Maxwell, C. W.		$30 Jan - Sep
12	Snellings, G. W.	Died 12 May 1932	$30 Jan – Apr$
13	Swift, T. M.	Died 18 Jan 1932 Pd. Widow Feb.	30 Jan – Mar
14	Thornton, J. W.		$30 Jan - Sep

1929 Widows Pension Roll

The following table presents the transcribed information in seven columns. The first column includes a consecutive number assigned to each pensioner, the second column is the name of the pensioner, the third column includes all of the nonpayment related information recorded by the clerk, and the last four columns include the pension amounts paid in each of the four quarters of 1929.

No.	Name	Remarks	1st Qtr	2nd Qtr	3rd Qtr	4th Qtr
1	Adams, Mrs. F. L.		$50	$50	$50	$50
2	Anderson, Sarah C.		$50	$50	$50	$50
3	Booth, Mrs. L. C.		$50	$50	$50	$50
4	Bowman, Mrs. A. E.		$50	$50	$50	$50
5	Brown, Mrs. N. S.		$50	$50	$50	$50
6	Burch, Mrs. Ida J.		$50	$50	$50	$50
7	Carpenter, Mrs. S. N.		$50	$50	$50	$50
8	Chandler, Mrs. L. E.		$50	$50	$50	$50
9	Charping, Mrs. S. E.		$50	$50	$50	$50
10	Cosby, Mrs. B. A.		$50	$50	$50	$50
11	Craft, Mrs. Rosa C.		$50	$50	$50	$50
12	Craft, Mrs. L. E.		$50	$50	$50	$50
13	Dixon, Mrs. Mollie S.		$50	$50	$50	$50
14	Fortson, Mrs. M. J.		$50	$50	$50	$50
15	Galloway, Mrs. S. F.		$50	$50	$50	$50
16	Ginn, Mrs. Julia A.	Died 18 Jul 1929	$50	$50	$50	
17	Ginn, Mrs. Mary	Died 21 Aug 1929	$50			

No.	Name	Remarks	1st Qtr	2nd Qtr	3rd Qtr	4th Qtr
18	Hewell, Mrs. S. A. C.		$50	$50	$50	$50
19	Hill, Mrs. Fannie		$50	$50	$50	$50
20	Hilley, Mrs. S. E.		$50	$50	$50	$50
21	Maxwell, Amanda C.		$50	$50	$50	$50
22	Maxwell, Mrs. L. M.		$50	$50	$50	$50
23	Maxwell, Mary H.		$50	$50	$50	$50
24	Mauldin, Permelia		$50	$50	$50	$50
25	Moss, Martha A.		$50	$50	$50	$50
26	McLanahan, Mrs. T. C.		$50	$50	$50	$50
27	McMullan, Mrs. J. L.		$50	$50	$50	$50
28	Rogers, Mrs. Mary E.		$50	$50	$50	$50
29	Roberts, Elizabeth J.		$50	$50	$50	$50
30	Seymour, Mrs. S.		$50	$50	$50	$50
31	Slay, Mrs. Frances		$50	$50	$50	$50
32	Smith, Mary Ann	Died 12 Jul 1929	$50			
33	Stilwell, Lillie Dora		$50	$50	$50	$50
34	Thornton, Sallie C.		$50	$50	$50	$50
35	Walker, Mrs. H. M.		$50	$50	$50	$50
36	Sanders, Ophelia		$50	$50	$50	$50
37	Warren, Antoinette		$50	$50	$50	$50
38	White, Mrs. L. M.		$50	$50	$50	$50
39	Whitman, Elizabeth	Died 2 May 1929	$50			
40	Willis, E. A.	Died 5 Jun 1929	$50			

No.	Name	Remarks	1st Qtr	2nd Qtr	3rd Qtr	4th Qtr
41	Willis, Mrs. L. G.		$50	$50	$50	$50

1930 Widows Pension Roll

The following table presents the transcribed information in seven columns. The first column includes a consecutive number assigned to each pensioner, the second column is the name of the pensioner, the third column includes all of the nonpayment related information recorded by the clerk, and the last four columns include the pension amounts paid in each of the four quarters of 1930.

No.	Name	Remarks	1st Qtr	2nd Qtr	3rd Qtr	4th Qtr
1	Adams, Mrs. F. L.		$50	$50	$50	$50
2	Anderson, Sara C.		$50	$50	$50	$50
3	Booth, Mrs. L. C.		$50	$50	$50	$50
4	Bowman, Mrs. A. E.		$50	$50	$50	$50
5	Brown, Mrs. N. S.	Died 6 Aug 1930	$50	$50		
6	Burch, Mrs. Ida J.		$50	$50	$50	$50
7	Carpenter, Mrs. S. N.		$50	$50	$50	$50
8	Chandler, Mrs. L. E.		$50	$50	$50	$50
9	Charping, Mrs. S. E.		$50	$50	$50	$50
10	Cosby, Mrs. B. A.		$50	$50	$50	$50
11	Craft, Mrs. Rosa C.		$50	$50	$50	$50
12	Craft, Mrs. L. E.		$50	$50	$50	$50
13	Dixon, Mrs. Mollie S.		$50	$50	$50	$50

No.	Name	Remarks	1st Qtr	2nd Qtr	3rd Qtr	4th Qtr
14	Fortson, Mrs. M. J.		$50	$50	$50	$50
15	Galloway, Mrs. S. F.		$50	$50	$50	$50
16	Hewell, Mrs. S. A. C.		$50	$50	$50	$50
17	Hill, Mrs. Fannie		$50	$50	$50	$50
18	Hilley, Mrs. S. E.		$50	$50	$50	$50
19	Maxwell, Mrs. Amanda C.		$50	$50	$50	$50
20	Maxwell, Mrs. L. M.	Died 1 Nov 1930	$50	$50	$50	
21	Maxwell, Mary H.		$50	$50	$50	$50
22	Mauldin, Permelia		$50	$50	$50	$50
23	Moss, Martha A.		$50	$50	$50	$50
24	McLanahan, Mrs. T. C.		$50	$50	$50	$50
25	McMullan, Mrs. J. L.	Died 4 Jul 1930	$50	$50		
26	Rogers, Mrs. Mary E.		$50	$50	$50	$50
27	Roberts, Elizabeth J.	Died 25 Oct 1930	$50	$50	$50	
28	Seymour, Mrs. S.		$50	$50	$50	$50
29	Slay, Mrs. Frances		$50	$50	$50	$50
30	Stilwell, Lillie Dora		$50	$50	$50	$50
31	Thornton, Sallie C.		$50	$50	$50	$50
32	Walker, Mrs. H. M.		$50	$50	$50	$50
33	Sanders, Ophelia		$50	$50	$50	$50
34	Warren, Antoinette		$50	$50	$50	$50
35	White, Mrs. L. M.		$50	$50	$50	$50

No.	Name	Remarks	1st Qtr	2nd Qtr	3rd Qtr	4th Qtr
36	Willis, Mrs. L. G.		$50	$50	$50	$50

1931 Widows Pension Roll

The following table presents the transcribed information in four columns. The first column includes a consecutive number assigned to each pensioner, the second column is the name of the pensioner, the third column includes all of the nonpayment related information recorded by the clerk, and the fourth column includes the pension amounts paid in each of the months of 1931.

No.	Name	Remarks	Months Paid
1	Adams, Mrs. F. L.		$30 Jan - Dec
2	Anderson, Sarah A.		$30 Jan - Dec
3	Booth, Mrs. L. C.		$30 Jan - Dec
4	Bowman, Mrs. A. E.		$30 Jan - Dec
5	Burch, Mrs. Ida J.	Died 17 Feb 1931	
6	Carpenter, Mrs. S. N.	Died 13 May 1931	$30 Jan - Feb
7	Chandler, Mrs. L. E.		$30 Jan - Dec
8	Charping, Mrs. S. E.		$30 Jan - Dec
9	Cosby, Mrs. B. A.		$30 Jan - Dec
10	Craft, Mrs. L. E.	Died 13 Mar 1931	
11	Craft, Mrs. Rosa C.		$30 Jan - Dec
12	Dixon, Mrs. Mollie S.		$30 Jan - Dec
13	Fortson, Mrs. M. J.	Died 5 Oct 1932 $20.00 Transferred Feb	$30 Jan - Dec
14	Galloway, Mrs. S. F.		$30 Jan - Dec
15	Hewell, Mrs. S. A. C.		$30 Jan - Dec
16	Hill, Mrs. Fannie		$30 Jan - Dec
17	Hilley, Mrs. S. E.		$30 Jan - Dec

No.	Name	Remarks	Months Paid
18	Maxwell, Mrs. Amanda		$30 Jan - Dec
19	Maxwell, Mrs. Mary H.		$30 Jan - Dec
20	Mauldin, Permelia		$30 Jan - Dec
21	Moss, Mrs. Martha A.		$30 Jan - Dec
22	McLanahan, Mrs. T. C.	Died 29 Oct 1931	$30 Jan – May, $30 Jul - Oct
23	Rogers, Mrs. Mary E.	Died 4 Aug 1931	$30 Jan – May $30 Aug
24	Seymour, Mrs. S.		$30 Jan - Dec
25	Slay, Mrs. Frances		$30 Jan - Dec
26	Stilwell, Lillie Dora		$30 Jan - Dec
27	Sanders, Mrs. Ophelia		$30 Jan - Dec
28	Thornton, Sallie C.		$30 Jan - Dec
29	Walker, Mrs. H. M.	Died 25 Jun 1931	$30 Jan - May
30	White, Mrs. L. M.		$30 Jan - Dec
31	Willis, Mrs. L. G.		$30 Jan - Dec
32	Warren, Antoinette	Died 3 Apr 1931	$30 Jan
33	Burden, Elizabeth P.	Widow of J. A. Burden	$30 Mar - Dec

1932 Widows Pension Roll

The following table presents the transcribed information in four columns. The first column includes a consecutive number assigned to each pensioner, the second column is the name of the pensioner, the third column includes all of the nonpayment related information recorded by the clerk, and the fourth column includes the pension amounts paid in each of the months of 1932.

No.	Name	Remarks	Months Paid
1	Adams, Mrs. F. L.		$30 Jan - Sep
2	Anderson, Sarah A.		$30 Jan - Sep
3	Burden, Elizabeth		$30 Jan - Sep
4	Booth, Mrs. L. C.		$30 Jan - Sep
5	Bowman, Mrs. A. E.		$30 Jan - Sep
6	Chandler, Mrs. L. E.		$30 Jan - Sep
7	Charping, Mrs. S. E.		$30 Jan - Sep
8	Cosby, Mrs. B. A.		$30 Jan - Sep
9	Craft, Mrs. Rosa C.		$30 Jan - Sep
10	Dixon, Mrs. Mollie S.		$30 Jan - Sep
11	Fortson, Mrs. M. J.	Died 5 Oct 1932	$30 Jan - Sep
12	Galloway, Mrs. S. F.		$30 Jan - Sep
13	Hewell, Mrs. S. A. C.		$30 Jan - Sep
14	Hill, Mrs. Fannie		$30 Jan - Sep
15	Hilley, Mrs. S. E.		$30 Jan - Sep
16	Maxwell, Mrs. Amanda		$30 Jan - Sep
17	Maxwell, Mrs. Mary H.		$30 Jan - Sep
18	Mauldin, Permelia		$30 Jan - Sep

No.	Name	Remarks	Months Paid
19	Moss, Mrs. Martha A.		$30 Jan - Sep
20	Seymour, Mrs. S.		$30 Jan - Sep
21	Slay, Mrs. Frances		$30 Jan - Sep
22	Stilwell, Lillie Dora		$30 Jan - Sep
23	Sanders, Mrs. Ophelia		$30 Jan - Sep
24	Thornton, Sallie C.		$30 Jan - Sep
25	White, Mrs. L. M.	Died 13 Apr 1932	$30 Jan – Apr
26	Willis, Mrs. L. G.		$30 Jan - Sep
27	Swift, Sarah E.	Died 17 Mar 1932	

1929-1930 Pension Roll

The following three entries on the last page of the original volume appear to be an overflow from the first two lists.

No.	Name	Remarks	Years Paid
	Childs, S. G.		$40 1929 1930
	Gulley, J. W.	Placed in Soldiers home 31 Mar 1930	$90 1929, $22.50 1930
	Hudson, W. A. C.	Died 6 Dec 1929	$90 1929

Volume III

Printed on the spine of the third original volume are the words *Pension Record*. The book consists of a series of printed tables for the clerk to use in recording the pensioners and his payments to them. However, the clerks only loosely followed the printed formats, instead frequently crossing out printed headings and replacing them with headings of their own, resulting in a series of twenty-three separate pension rolls in approximate chronological order.

1921-1923 Old Pension Roll

The following table presents the transcribed pension roll in four columns, the name of the soldier in the first column, his post office address in the second, the pension amount paid each year in the third, and all other information in the fourth column, titled Remarks.

Name	Address	Amount Paid	Remarks
Adams, W. H. H.	#6, Elberton, Ga.	$125 1921, $100 1922-1923	
~~Bringhurst, Ed S.~~	~~Elberton, Ga.~~	~~$125 1921,~~ ~~$100 1922~~-Pd. later $100 1923	~~Left State 1921 Miss.~~
Bailey, F. O.	#8, Elberton, Ga.	$125 1921, $100 1922-1923	
Butler, T. N.	#1, Bowman, Ga.	$125 1921, $100 1922-1923	
~~Brown, J. R.~~	~~#9, Elberton, Ga.~~	~~$125 1921,~~ ~~$100 1922-1923~~	~~Died 29 Jun 1923~~
Brooks, C. T.	% White Bros. Watkinsville, Ga.	$100 1921 Refund	Dead 1921
Brown, J. M.	#3, Covington, Ga.	$125 1921, $100 1922	Pd. Widow Married 3 Jan 1894 Mrs. Elizabeth Brown Dead 8 Jun 1922
Bell, G. S.	#1, Tignall, Ga.	$125 1921, $100 1922-1923	
~~Bailey, L. L.~~	~~Elberton, Ga.~~	~~$125 1921,~~ ~~$100 1922-1923~~	~~Pd. Funeral Expenses Dead 1923~~
~~Brown, B. D.~~	~~Elberton, Ga.~~	~~$125 1921,~~ ~~$100 1922-1923~~	
Conwell, J. D.	Lavonia, Ga.	$100 1921-1923	

Name	Address	Amount Paid	Remarks
Cleveland, R. W.	#3, Elberton, Ga.	$125 1921, $100 1922-1923	
Caldwell, A. V.	#7, Elberton, Ga.	$125 1921, $100 1922-1923	
Childs, J. B.	#1, Middleton, Ga.	$125 1921, $100 1922-1923	
Charping, W. L.	#9, Elberton, Ga.	$125 1921, $100 1922-1923	Co H, 30 Ga Paid to W. L. Charping 29 Apr 1921 S. C. Charping, Widow Died 13 Aug 1921
Dixon, A. W.	#9, Elberton, Ga.	$125 1921, $100 1922-1923	
Dixon, S. W.	#1, Middleton, Ga.	$125 1921, $100 1922-1923	
Dixon, Abram	Elberton, Ga.	$125 1921, $100 1922-1923	
Davis, W. P.	Oglesby, Ga.	$125 1921, $100 1922-1923	
Eavenson, J. W.	Bowman, Ga.	$125 1921, $100 1922-1923	
Fleming, J. H.	#1, Middleton, Ga.	$125 1921, $100 1922-1923	
Fleming, Lawrence C.	#8, Elberton, Ga.	$125 1921, $100 1922-1923	
Guest, S. B.	#8, Elberton, Ga. Wilson Av 189 Courtland St. Atlanta, Ga	$125 1921, $100 1922-1923	Brown Bros Sons Transferred
Gulley, J. W.	1140 Boulevard St., c/o Joe Smith,	$125 1921, $100 1922-1923	

Name	Address	Amount Paid	Remarks
	Athens		
Gaines, W. S.	Elberton, Ga.	$125 1921, $100 1922-1923	
Gaines, P. C. #2	#2, Elberton, Ga.	$125 1921, $100 1922-1923	
Hill, T. M.	#1, Middleton, Ga.	$125 1921 109 Brown Bros Pd. Widow	Insolvent 27 May 1922
Higginbotham, J. H.	245 Gordon St. Elberton, Ga.	$125 1921, $100 1922-1923	Pd. to Mrs. T. L. Higginbotham, Widow Died 23 Dec 1923
Hall, A. O.	#1, Middleton, Ga.	$125 1921 Paid to G. O. Hall Clark Edwards, Jr. Ardy, F. E.	Insolvent No widow Died Oct 1921
Hudson, W. A. C.	#7, Elberton, Ga.	$125 1921, $100 1922-1923	
Hansard, J. R.	#2, Elberton, Ga.	$125 1921 Refund	Solvent Died 4 May 1922 No widow
Hamm, P. H.	#1, Elberton, Ga.	$125 1921, $100 1922-1923	
Heard, J. L.	#1, Elberton, Ga.	$125 1921 $100 1922 Pd. F. expenses	Died 17 Jun 1922 No widow
Johnson, J. N.	#5, Elberton, Ga.	$125 1921, $100 1922-1923	
Johnson, A. V.	#1, Middleton, Ga.	$125 1921, $100 1922-1923	
Maxwell, C. W.	Bowman, Ga.	$125 1921, $100 1922-1923	

68

Name	Address	Amount Paid	Remarks
Mabrey, T. W.	32 Gordon, St. Elberton, Ga.	$125 1921, $100 1922-1923	Trans 10 Dec 1923 Hart Co.
Martin, P. C.	#1, Middleton, Ga.		Insolvent
Powell, J. F.	Elberton, Ga.	$125 Returned	Insolvent No widow Dead Jan 1921
Snellings, G. W	#7, Elberton, Ga.	$125 1921, $100 1922-1923	
Snellings, G. T.	#1, Tignall, Ga.	$125 1921, $100 1922-1923	
Scoggins, J. W.	Bowman, Ga.	$125 1921 $98 1922 Refund $2 Pd. Funeral Expenses	Insolvent No widow Dead Jan 1922
Sanders, W. A.	#2, Elberton, Ga.	$125 1921, $100 1922-1923	
Sanders, T. W.	Bowman, Ga.	$125 1921, $100 1922-1923	
Slay, G. F.	#7, Elberton, Ga.	$125 1921, $100 1922-1923	
Swift, T. M.	Elberton, Ga.	$125 1921, $100 1922-1923	
Tate, Jno. S.	378 Tustin St. Elberton, Ga.	$125 1921, $100 1922-1923	
Wansley, Thos. N.	#2, Elberton, Ga.	$125 1921, $100 1922-1923	Died 4 Feb 1824
White., A. L.	#2, Royston, Ga.	$125 1921, $100 1922 Pd. Funeral Expenses	Died 26 Jun 1922
Willis, T. B. F.	#1, Elberton, Ga.	$125 1921 Pd. to Elizabeth Ann	Co C, 15 Ga

Name	Address	Amount Paid	Remarks
		Willis	Died 2 Jul 1921

1920-1923 New Pension Roll

The following table presents the transcribed pension roll in five columns, the first column the year the soldier was added to the pension roll, the second the name of the pensioner, the third his post office address, the fourth the pension amount paid each year, and the fifth all other information recorded by the clerk.

When Added	Name	Address	Amount Paid	Remarks
1920	Adams, S. A.	Elberton, Ga. #3	$100 1920 $125 1921	
1920	Adams, W. M.	Elberton, Ga. #6	$100 1923 Returned	No widow Solvent Died 1921
1920	Adams, T. R.	Elberton, Ga.	$100 1923 Returned	Widow Did not make application before Nov 1919 Died Sep 1919
1920	Brown, S. G.	Bowman, Ga.	$100 1920 $125 1921 $100 1923	
1920	Bryan, Jasper	Elberton, Ga. #5	$100 1920 $125 1921	
1920	Ginn, D. L.	Bowman, Ga.	$100 1920 $125 1921 $125 Returned Widow drawing $100	Paid to Mrs. Mary L. Ginn Died

70

When Added	Name	Address	Amount Paid	Remarks
1920	~~Hall, F. M.~~	~~Bowman, Ga.~~	$100 1923 $100 Returned	No widow Solvent 1921
1920	Harper, J. M.	Elberton, Ga.	$100 1920 $125 1921	Left widow Died 17 Mar 1922
1921	Heard, E. B.	#1, Middleton, Ga.	$125 1921	
1920	Hendrick, F. M.	Bowman, Ga.	$100 1920 $125 1921	Dead
1920	Jones, J. M.	Elberton, Ga. #4	$100 1920 $125 1921	
1920	Jones, Thos. A.	Elberton, Ga.	$100 1920 $125 1921	Dead
1920	Kelley, W. T.	Elberton, Ga. #1	$100 1920 $125 1921	
1920	Mattox, N. M.	Elberton, Ga.	$100 1920 $125 1921	Dead
1920	Maxwell, Chandler	Dewey Rose, Ga. #2	$100 1920 $125 1921	
1920	Maxwell, Daniel J.	Dewey Rose, Ga. #2	$100 1920 $125 1921	
1920	McMullen, J. L.	Elberton, Ga. #6	$100 1920 $125 1921	Co G, 37 Ga Left widow Paid Widow Yellow Blard #225[00] Died 11 Nov 1921
1920	Norman, E. B	Dewey Rose, Ga. #1	$100 1920 $125 1921	Died 14 Mar 1922
1920	Oglesby, D. B. (P)	Elberton, Ga.	$100 1920	

When Added	Name	Address	Amount Paid	Remarks
			$125 1921	
1920	Ray, W. R.	Bowman, Ga.	$100 1920 $125 1921	
1920	Roberts, W. C.	Bowman, Ga.	$100 1920 $125 1921	
1920	Rice, W. J.	Bowman, Ga.	$225 Returned	No widow. Solvent. Died May 1920
1920	Snellings, W. J.	Elberton, Ga	$100 1920 $125 1921	
1920	Seymour, J. G.	Dewey Rose, Ga.	$100 1920 $125 1921	Died Apr 1923
1920	Teasley, J. A.	Elberton, Ga. #6	$100 1920 $125 1921	
1920	Thornton, J. W.	Elberton, Ga. #6	$100 1920 $125 1921	
1920	Thornton, T. D.	Bowman, Ga.	$100 1920 $125 1921	No widow. Solvent. Died 6 Apr 1922
1920	Tate, W. E.	Elberton, Ga. #13	$100 1920 $125 1921	
1921	Willis, T. F.	Elberton, Ga. #5	$125 1921 $100 1922	
1921	Childs, S. G.	Elberton, Ga. #1	$125 1921 $100 1922	
1922	Cochran, G. W.	Dewey Rose, Ga. #2	$100 1922	Co F, 37 Ga 14 Dec 1921 Stephens Co., Ga.

1924 Pension Roll

The following table presents the transcribed information in three columns. The first column contains the name of the soldier, the second column contains the pension amount paid in 1924, and the third column contains all of the other information recorded by the clerk.

Name	Amount Paid	Remarks
Adams, W. H. H.	$125 1924	Dead
Adams, S. A.	$125 1924	
Bailey, F. O.	$125 1924	
Bell, G. S.	$125 1924	4 Jan 1926
Bringhurst, Ed S.	$100 1924	Refund Dead
Brown, B. D.	$125 1924	Died 7 Aug 1925
Brown, J. R.	$125 1924	Mrs. Mary E. Brown, Box 3, Rt. 9 Died 29 Jun 1925
Brown, S. G.	$125 1924	
Bryan, Jasper	$125 1924	
Burden, J. A.	$125 1924	
Butler, T. N.	$100 1924	Refund Died 19 Jul 1924
Caldwell, A. V.	$125 1924	
Cochran, T. W.	$125 1924	Died
Childs, J. B.	$125 1924	
Childs, S. G.	$125 1924	
Cleveland, R. W.	$125 1924	
Conwell, J. D.	$125 1924	

Name	Amount Paid	Remarks
Davis, W. P.	$125 1924	Dead
Dixon, Abram	$125 1924	
Dixon, A. W.	$100 1924 Pd. Funeral Expenses	Died 11 Feb 1924
Dixon, S. W.	$125 1924	Died 8 Apr 1926
Eavenson, J. W.	$125 1924	
Fleming, J. H.	$125 1924	
Fleming, Lawrence	Returned	Dead 21 Apr 1924
Gaines, P. C.	$125 1924	
Gaines, W. S.	$125 1924	
Guest, S. B.	$100 1924 Pd. Funeral Expenses	1140 Boulevard c/o Joe Smith, Athens, Ga. unless by order Died 20 Mar 1924
Gulley, J. W.	$125 1924	
Hamm, P. H.	$125 1924	
Heard, E. B.	$125 1924	
Hudson, W. A. C.	$125 1924	
Johnson, A. V.	$100 1924 Returned	29 Sep 1924
Johnson, J. N.	$125 1924	Dewey Rose, Ga. #2
Jones, J. M.	$125 1924	
Kelley, W. T.	$125 1924	
Mattox, N. M.	Returned	Dead Oct 1923
Maxwell, Chandler	$125 1924	

75

Name	Amount Paid	Remarks
Maxwell, C. W.	$125 1924	
Maxwell, Daniel J.	$125 1924	
Norman, E. B.	$125 1924	Died 14 Mar 1926
Oglesby, D. P.	$125 1924	
Ray, W. R.	Returned	Dead 19 Mar 1924
Roberts, W. C.	$125 1924	
Sanders, W. A.	$125 1924	Died 26 Mar 1925
Sanders, T. W.	$125 1924	
Slay, G. F.	$125 1924	
Snellings, G. T.	$125 1924	Died 1925
Snellings, G. W.	$125 1924	
Snellings, W. J.	$125 1924	
Swift, T. M.	$125 1924	
Tate, Jno. S.	$125 1924	Died 13 Oct 1925
Tate, W. E.	$125 1924	
Teasley, J. A.	$125 1924	
Thornton, J. W.	$125 1924	
Wandley, Thos. N.	$100 1924 Paid Funeral Expenses	Died 4 Feb 1924
Willis, T. F.	$125 1924	

1926 Pension Roll

The following table presents the transcribed pension roll in eight columns, a consecutive number assigned to each soldier in the first column, the name of the soldier in the second, and his post office address and all other information, except payments, recorded by the clerk in the third column. The pension amounts paid for each quarter of 1926 are in the next four columns. The last, or eighth, column contains the total amount due each pensioner from previous years, but not yet paid.

No.	Name	Address and Remarks	1st Qtr	2nd Qtr	3rd Qtr	4th Qtr	Past Due
1	Adams, S. A.	Elberton, Ga. #3	$50	$50	$50	$50	$460
2	Bailey, F. O.	Elberton, Ga. #8	$50	$50	$50	$50	$260
3	Bell, G. S.	Tignall, Ga. Died before 1st Quarter 4 Jan 1926 Insolvent $50 Returned					
4	Brown, S. G.	Bowman, Ga.	$50	$50	$50	$50	$360
5	Bryan, Jasper	Dewey Rose, Ga. #1	$50	$50	$50	$50	$460
6	Burden, J. A.	Comes, Ga.	$50	$50	$50	$50	$260
7	Caldwell, A. V.	Elberton, Ga. #7	$50	$50	$50	$50	$260
8	Childs, J. B.	Middleton, Ga. #1	$50	$50	$50	$50	
9	Childs, S. G.	Elberton, Ga. #1	$50	$50	$50	$50	$260
10	Cleveland, R. W.	Elberton, Ga.	$50	$50	$50	$50	$260
11	Conwell, J. D.	Lavonia, Ga.	$50	$50	$50	$50	$260
12	Davis, W. P.	Oglesby, Ga.	$50	$50	$50		$260
13	Dixon, Abram	Elberton, Ga.	$50	$50	$50	$50	$260
14	Dixon, S. W.	Middleton, Ga. Died after 1st	$50				

No.	Name	Address and Remarks	1st Qtr	2nd Qtr	3rd Qtr	4th Qtr	Past Due
		Quarter Wife added 2nd Quarter (1926)					
15	Eavenson, J. W.	Bowman, Ga.	$50	$50	$50	$50	$260
16	Fleming, J. H.	Middleton, Ga. #1	$50	$50	$50	$50	$260
17	Gaines, P. C.	Elberton, Ga. #2	$50	$50	$50	$50	$260
18	Gaines, W. S.	Elberton, Ga.	$50	$50	$50	$50	$260
19	Gulley, J. W.	Elberton, Ga.	$50	$50	$50	$50	$260
20	Hamm, P. H.	Elberton, Ga. #1	$50	$50	$50	$50	$260
21	Heard, E. B.	Middleton, Ga.	$50	$50	$50	$50	$460
22	Hudson, W. A. C.	Elberton, Ga. #7	$50	$50	$50	$50	$260
23	Johnson, J. N.	Elberton, Ga.	$50	$50	$50	$50	$260
24	Jones, J. M.	Elberton, Ga. #4	$50	$50	$50	$50	$460
25	Kelley, W. T.	Elberton, Ga. #1	$50	$50	$50	$50	$460
26	Maxwell, Chandler	Dewey Rose, Ga. #2 Died after 1st Quarter, Wife added 2nd Quarter	$50				
27	Maxwell, C. W.	Bowman, Ga.	$50	$50	$50	$50	4260
28	Norman, E. B.	Dewey Rose, Ga. Died after 1st Quarter, Wife added 2nd Quarter 1926	$50				
29	Oglesby, D. P.	Elberton, Ga.	$50	$50	$50	$50	$460
30	Roberts, W. C.	Bowman, Ga. 25th Ga Cav	$50	$50	$50	$50	$360

No.	Name	Address and Remarks	1st Qtr	2nd Qtr	3rd Qtr	4th Qtr	Past Due
31	Sanders, J. W.	Bowman, Ga.	$50	$50	$50	$50	$260
32	Slay, G. F.	Elberton, Ga. #7	$50	$50	$50	$50	$260
33	Snellings, G. W.	Elberton, Ga. #7	$50	$50	$50	$50	$260
34	Snellings, W. J.	Elberton, Ga.	$50	$50	$50	$50	$460
35	Swift, T. M.	Elberton, Ga.	$50	$50	$50	$50	$260
36	Tate, W. E.	Elberton, Ga. #12	$50	$50	$50	$50	$460
37	Teasley, J. A.	Elberton, Ga. #6	$50	$50	$50	$50	$360
38	Thornton, J. W.	Dewey Rose, Ga. #2	$50	$50	$50	$50	$360
39	Willis, T. F.	Elberton, Ga. #5	$50	$50	$50	$50	$360

1927 Pension Roll

The following table presents the transcribed pension roll in six columns, the first column a consecutive number assigned to each soldier, the second the name of the pensioner, the third his post office address, the fourth and fifth the pension amount paid the first two quarters of 1927, and the sixth all other information recorded by the clerk.

No.	Name	Address	1st Qtr	2nd Qtr	Remarks
1	Adams, S. A.	Elberton, Ga.	$50	$50	
2	Bailey, F. O.	Elberton, Ga.	$50	$50	
3	Brown, S. G.	Bowman, Ga.	$50	$50	
4	Bryan, Jasper	Dewey Rose, Ga.	$50	$50	
5	Burden, J. A.	Hull, Ga.	$50	$50	Died 2 Aug 1927
6	Caldwell, A. V.	Elberton, Ga.	$50	$50	
7	Childs, J. B.	Middleton, Ga.	$50	$50	
8	Childs, S. G.	Elberton, Ga.	$50	$50	
9	Cleveland, R. W.	Elberton, Ga.	$50	$50	
10	Conwell, J. D.	Lavonia, Ga.	$50	$50	
11	Eavenson, J. W.	Bowman, Ga.	$50	$50	
12	Fleming, J. H.	Middleton, Ga.	$50	$50	
13	Gaines, P. C.	Elberton, Ga.	$50	$50	
14	Gaines, W. S.	Elberton, Ga.	$50	$50	
15	Gulley, J. W.	Elberton, Ga.	$50	$50	
16	Hamm, P. H.	Elberton, Ga.	$50	$50	
17	Heard, E. B.	Elberton, Ga.	$50	$50	
18	Hudson, W. A. C.	Elberton, Ga.	$50	$50	

No.	Name	Address	1st Qtr	2nd Qtr	Remarks
19	Jones, J. M.	Elberton, Ga.	$50	$50	
20	Kelley, W. T.	Elberton, Ga.	$50	$50	
21	Maxwell, C. W.	Bowman, Ga.	$50	$50	
22	Oglesby, D. P.	Elberton, Ga.	$50	$50	
23	Roberts, W. C.	Bowman, Ga.	$50		Co M, 25 Ga Cav Died 13 May 1927 Refunded Second Quarter 21 May 1927
24	Sanders, T. W.	Bowman, Ga.	$50	$50	
25	Slay, G. F.	Elberton, Ga.	$50	$50	
26	Snellings, G. W.	Elberton, Ga.	$50	$50	
27	Snellings, W. J.	Elberton, Ga.	$50		Died Solvent 26 Feb 1927
28	Swift, T. M.	Elberton, Ga.	$50	$50	
29	Tate, W. E.	Elberton, Ga.	$50	$50	
30	Teasley, J. A.	Elberton, Ga.	$50	$50	Died 21 Jan 1928
31	Thornton, J. W.	Dewey Rose, Ga.	$50	$50	
32	Willis, T. F.	Elberton, Ga.	$50	$50	

1928 Pension Roll

The following table presents the transcribed pension roll in five columns, the first column the name of the pensioner, the second, third, and fourth the pension amount paid the first three quarters of 1928, and the fifth all other information recorded by the clerk.

Name	1st Qtr	2nd Qtr	3rd Qtr	Remarks
Adams, S. A.	$50	$50	$50	
Bailey, F. O.	$50	$50	$50	
Brown, S. G.	$50	$50	$50	
Burden, J. A.	$50	$50	$50	
Bryan, Jasper				Dead. Returned 6 Jun 1928. Solvent. No widow.
Burden, J. A. (Entered Twice}				
Caldwell, A. V.	$50	$50		Returned 16 Nov 1928 Died 23 Aug 1928
Childs, J. B.	$50	$50	$50	
Childs, S. G.	$50	$50	$50	
Cleveland, R. W.	$50	$50	$50	
Conwell, J. D.	$50	$50	$50	
Eavenson, J. W.	$50	$50	$50	
Fleming, J. H.	$50	$50	$50	
Gaines, W. S.	$50	$50	$50	
Gulley, J. W.	$50	$50	$50	
Hamm, P. H.	$50	$50	$50	
Heard, E. B	$50	$50	$50	

Name	1st Qtr	2nd Qtr	3rd Qtr	Remarks
Hudson, W. A. C.	$50	$50	$50	
Jones, J. M.	$50	$50	$50	
Kelley, W. T.	$50	$50		Died
Maxwell, C. W.	$50	$50	$50	
Oglesby, D. P.	$50	$50	$50	
Sanders, T. W.	$50			Widow added. Died May 1928.
Slay, T. F.	$50	$50	$50	Widow added. Died 18 Oct 1928
Snellings, G. W.	$50	$50	$50	
Swift, F. M.	$50	$50	$50	
Tate, W. E.	$50	$50	$50	
Thornton, J. W.	$50	$50	$50	
Teasley, J. A.				Died 21 Jan 1928. No money sent down. Widow
Willis, T. F.	$50	$50	$50	

Correspondence

The following two letters have been inserted into the original record volume.

State of Georgia
Pension Department
Atlanta

John W. Clark
Commissioner of Pensions

August 28, 1926

Hon. Clark Edwards, Jr.
Ordinary of Elbert County
Elberton, Georgia

Dear Judge:

I have this day approved the application of Mrs. S. A. E. Almond, the widow of John Benjamin Almond, deceased Confederate soldier, to be placed on the Pension Roll of Georgia in her own right and have added her name to the Pension Rolls of this State. You may place Mrs. Almond's name on your roll to be paid the pension for 1926.

Yours very truly,

John W. Clark
Commissioners of Pensions

State of Georgia
Pension Department
Atlanta

John W. Clark
Commissioner of Pensions

October 19, 1925

Hon. Clark Edwards, Jr.
Ordinary of Elbert County
Elberton, Georgia

Dear Judge:

The application of Mrs. Amanda Catherine Maxwell, the widow of Daniel J. Maxwell, deceased pensioner, has this day been approved by me. You may place her name on your roll for 1926 payment.

Yours very truly,

John W. Clark
Commissioners of Pensions

1924-1925 Pension Roll

The following table presents the transcribed pension roll in six columns, the first column a consecutive number assigned to each soldier, the second the name of the pensioner, the third his post office address, the fourth and fifth the pension amount paid each year, and the fifth all other information recorded by the clerk.

No.	Name	Address	1924	1925	Remarks
1	Adams, W. H. H.	#6, Elberton, Ga.	~~100~~	100	Dead
2	Adams, S. A.	#3, Elberton, Ga.	~~100~~	140	
3	Bailey, F. O.	#8, Elberton, Ga.	~~100~~	140	
4	Bell, G. S.	Tignall, Ga.	~~100~~	140	c/o J. A. Maxwell, Elberton, Ga. Died 3 Jan 1926
5	Brown, B. D.	Elberton, Ga.	~~100~~	100	Died 7 Aug 1925
6	Brown, J. R.	Elberton, Ga.	~~100~~	100	Died 29 Jun 1925
7	Brown, S. G.	Bowman, Ga.	~~100~~	140	
8	Bryan, Jasper	#5, Elberton, Ga.	~~100~~	140	
9	Burden, J. A.	#3, Hull, Ga.	~~100~~	140	
10	Caldwell, A. V.	#7, Elberton, Ga.	~~100~~	140	Died 2 Aug 1928
11	Cochran, T. W.	#2, Dewey Rose, Ga.	~~100~~	100	Co F, 37 Ga 19 Dec 1921 Stephens County Dead
12	Childs, J. B.	#1, Middleton, Ga.	~~100~~	140	
13	Childs, S. G.	#1, Elberton, Ga.	~~100~~	140	
14	Cleveland, R. W.	Church St. Elberton, Ga.	~~100~~	140	
15	Conwell, J. D.	Lavonia, Ga.	~~100~~	140	

No.	Name	Address	1924	1925	Remarks
16	Davis, W. P.		~~100~~	140	Dead
17	Dixon, Abram	Elberton, Ga. c/o Will Reagan	~~100~~	140	
18	Dixon, S. W.	#1, Middleton, Ga.		140	Died 8 Apr
19	Eavenson, J. W.	Bowman, Ga.		140	
20	Fleming, J. H.	#1, Middleton, Ga.		140	
21	Gaines, P. C.	#6, Elberton, Ga.		140	
22	Gaines, W. S.	Elberton, Ga.		140	
23	Gulley, J. W.	Elberton, Ga.		140	
24	Hamm, P. H.	#1, Elberton, Ga.		140	
25	Heard, E. B.	#1, Middleton, Ga.		140	
26	Hudson, W. A. C.	#7, Elberton, Ga.		140	
27	Johnson, J. N.			140	
28	Jones, J. M.	#4, Elberton, Ga.		140	
29	Kelley, W. T.	#1, Elberton, Ga.		140	
30	Maxwell, Chandler	#2, Dewey Rose, Ga.		140	
31	Maxwell, C. W.			140	
32	~~Maxwell, David J.~~	#2, Dewey Rose, Ga.		100	Died 29 Aug 1925
33	~~Norman, E. B.~~	Dewey Rose, Ga.		140	Died 14 Mar 1926
34	Oglesby, D. P.	Elberton, Ga.		140	
35	Roberts, W. C.	Bowman, Ga.		140	
36	~~Sanders, W. A.~~	#2, Elberton, Ga.		100	Died 26 Mar 1925 paid Mrs. W. A.

No.	Name	Address	1924	1925	Remarks
					Sanders
37	Slay, G. F.	#7, Elberton, Ga.			
38	~~Snellings, G. F.~~	Tignall, Ga.		140	Died 1925 Solvent Returned June 1925
39	Snellings, G. W.	#7, Elberton, Ga.		140	
40	Snellings, W. J.	Elberton, Ga. College Ave.		140	
41	Swift, T. M.	Elberton, Ga.		140	
42	~~Tate, Jno. S.~~	Elberton, Ga. Justin St.		100	Died 13 Oct 1925
43	Tate, W. E.	#4, Elberton, Ga.		140	
44	Teasley, J. A.	#6, Elberton, Ga.		140	
45	Thornton, J. W.	#6, Elberton, Ga.		140	
46	Willis, T. F.	#5, Elberton, Ga.		140	
47	Sanders, T. W.	Bowman, Ga.		140	

1921-1923 Widows Old Pension Roll

The following table presents the transcribed pension roll in six columns, the first column the name of the pensioner, the second her post office address, the third, fourth, and fifth the pension amount paid each year, and the six all other information recorded by the clerk.

Name	Address	1921	1922	1923	Remarks
Adams, Parthenia J.	c/o A. C. Adams Bowman, Ga.	125	100	100	
Anderson, Sarah A.	32, Elberton, Ga.	125	100	100	
Borden, Annie E.	Bowman, Ga. Notify J. C. Booth	125	100	100	
Booth, L. C.	#1, Dewey Rose, Ga.	125	100	100	
Brough, E. T.					Moved out of State 1920. South Carolina
Brown, Martha A.	Bowman, Ga.	125	100	100	
Bowman, A. E.	#1, Middleton, Ga.	125	100	100	
Brown, S. C.	437 McIntosh St. Elberton, Ga.	125	100	100	
Bond, Lucy C.	R. R. St. Elberton, Ga.	125	100	100	
Burden, S. C.	c/o J. G. Brown Dewey Rose	125	100	100	
Brown, N. S.	#7, S. M. Brown #2 Point Peter, Ga.	125	100	100	
Burriss, Ann		125	100	100	
Brown, Winnie A.	[faint]				Transferred 31 Dec 1924 to Madison County, Ga.

Name	Address	1921	1922	1923	Remarks
Craft, Rosa C.	c/o Mrs W. M. Bonds Elberton, Ga.	125	100	100	
Clark, Sallie J.	1833 Fenwick St. Augusta, Ga.	125	100	100	
Cox, M. A.	Elberton, Ga.	125	100	100	
Carpenter, H. D.	#6	125	100	100	
Cosby, B. A.	Elberton, Ga.	125	100	100	
Craft, L. E.	c/o A. L. Burtin #1, Dewey Rose, Ga.	125	100	100	
Colvard, Martha P.	Bowman, Ga.	125			Co G, 37 Ga Paid Clark Edwards, Jr. Paid F. Ex. Died 20 Feb 1921 Insolvent
Cunningham, M. E.	Dewey, Rose, Ga.	125	100	100	
Sanders, Alpha	#1, Elberton, Ga.	125	100	100	
Sanders, Mary A.	#6, Elberton, Ga.	125	100	100	Died 29 May 1925
Scarborough, C. W.	Royston, Ga.				Died Sep 1920
Smith, C. E.	#1, Elberton, Ga.	125	100	100	Pd. Funeral Expenses. Died 1923
Seymour, S.	c/o J. W. Seymour Tignall, Ga.	125	100	100	
Smith, Jennie	S. Oliver St. Elberton, Ga.	125	100	100	
Smith, Nancy E.	Mat Maxwell	125	100	100	
Snellings, Frances	Flatwoods	125	100	100	

Name	Address	1921	1922	1923	Remarks
L.					
Thornton, Sallie C.	C. B. Thornton Mother #5, Elberton, Ga.	125	100	100	
Thornton, S. E.	c/o Tom Thornton 32, Dewey Rose, Ga.	125	100	100	
White, L. M.	Elberton, Ga.	125	100	100	
Whitaker, Mary	Bowman, Ga.	125	100	100	
Whitman, Elizabeth	#7, Elberton, Ga. A. M. Hill Hardwood, Ga.	125	100	100	

1920-1923 Widows New Pension Roll

The following table presents the transcribed pension roll in seven columns, the first column the year the widow was added to the pension roll, the second the name of the pensioner, the third her post office address, the fourth, fifth, and sixth the pension amount paid each year, and the seventh all other information recorded by the clerk.

When Added	Name	Address	1920	1921	1923	Remarks
1920	~~Mize, Nancy C.~~	~~Dewey Rose, Ga., #1~~			~~100~~	~~Returned~~ ~~Died 1921~~ ~~Solvent~~
1920	McLanahan, T. C.	Elberton, Ga.	100	125	100	
1920	Mauldin, Permelia	Middleton, Ga., #1	100	125		
1920	McCurry, Susan B.	Elberton, Ga.	100	125		26 Mar 1926
1922	Maxwell, L. M. w/o Joe Maxwell	Elberton, Ga., #6				Ga. Militia Mrs. Kitty Maxwell
1923	McMullan, Mrs. J. L.					
1920	~~Nash, Rachel F.~~	~~Elberton, Ga., #12~~ Bet 61 #2 c/o John Yeargin [faint]	100	125		Died 12 Dec 1925
1921	~~Rhodes, A. E.~~	~~Elberton, Ga.~~		95^{25}		Pd. Clark Edwards and F. Ex. 29^{75} Died 28 Jul 1921
1920	Rogers, Mary E.	Elberton, Ga.	100	125		
1920	Smith, Mattie A.	~~#1, Milan, Ga.~~ ~~Nov 1922~~	100	125		Pitts, Ga., #1 Wilcox County

When Added	Name	Address	1920	1921	1923	Remarks
1920	Thornton, Lucinda J.	Elberton, Ga.	100	125		#225 Refunded Died 16 Dec 1921 Solvent
1920	Turman, Jane E.	Middleton, Ga., #1	100	125		Pd. Clark Edwards, Jr. and F. E. D. 17 Jan 1921 Insolvent
1921	Vickery, L. E.	Bowman, Ga.		125	100	
1920	Walker, H. M.	Bowman, Ga.	100	125		

1924 Widows Pension Roll

The following table presents the transcribed pension roll in four columns, the first column the name of the pensioner, the second and third the pension amount paid in 1924, and the fourth all other information recorded by the clerk. Apparently, two separate payments were made during the year.

Name	1924	1924	Remarks
Craft, L. E.	100	25	
Craft, Rosa C.	100	25	
Crawford, M. L.			Returned. Dead 1923
Cunningham, M. E.	100	25	
Fortson, M. J.	100	25	
Fortson, S. B.	100	25	Dead
Galloway, S. F.	100	25	
Ginn, Julia A.	100	25	
Ginn, Mary	100	25	
Goss, Cora A.	100	25	Died 30 May 1926
Hammond, Nancy F.	100	25	Died Nov 1924
Harper, Mrs. Sarah M.	100	25	Died 22 Feb 1926
Hewell, S. A. C.	100	25	
Hill, Mrs. Fannie	100	25	c/o J. W. Chapman, Hartwell #2
Hilley, S. E.	100	25	
Jones, M.	100		Died 7 Oct 1924
Jones, Miley A.	100	25	
Maxwell, L. M.	100	25	

Name	1924	1924	Remarks
Mauldin, Permelia	100	25	
Warren, Antoinette	100	25	
Webb, Mary E.	100	25	
~~Whitaker, Mary~~	100	25	Died 4 May 1926
White, L. M.	100	25	
Whitman, Elizabeth	100	25	A. M. Hill Heardmont
Willis, E. A.	100	25	
Willis, E. G.	100	25	

1925 Widows Pension Roll

The following table presents the transcribed pension roll in four columns, the first column the name of the pensioner, the second and third the pension amount paid in 1924, and the fourth all other information recorded by the clerk. Again apparently, two separate payments were made during the year.

Name	1925	1925	Remarks
Ginn, Mary	100	40	
Goss, Cora A.	100	40	
Harper, Mrs. Sara	100	40	Died 22 Feb 1926
Hewell, S. A. C.	100	40	
Hill, Mrs. Fannie	100	40	
Hilley, S. E.	100	40	
Jones, Miley A.	100	40	
Maxwell, L. M.	100	40	
Mauldin, Permelia	100	40	
Moss, Martha A.	100	40	
McCurry, Susan B.	100	40	Died 26 Mar 1926
McLanahan, T. C.	100	40	
McMullan, J. R.	100	40	
Nash, Rachel F.	100	40	Died 27 Dec 1925
Rogers, Mary E.	100	40	
Sanders, Mary A.	100		Died 29 May 1925
Seymour, S.	100	40	
Smith, Jenny	100	40	

Name	1925	1925	Remarks
Smith, Mattie A.	100	40	Funeral Ex. Died 1925
Snellings, Frances L.	100	40	
Thornton, Sallie C.	100	40	
Thornton, S. E.	100	40	Died
Walker, H. M.	100	40	
Warren, Antoinette	100	40	

1926 Widows Pension Roll

The following table presents the transcribed pension roll in eight columns, a consecutive number assigned to each widow in the first column, the name of the widow in the second, and her post office address and all other information, except payments, recorded by the clerk in the third column. The pension amounts paid for each quarter of 1926 are in the next four columns. The last, or eighth, column contains the total amount due each pensioner from previous years, but not yet paid.

No.	Name	Address and Remarks	1st Qtr	2nd Qtr	3rd Qtr	4th Qtr	Past Due
1	Adams, Mrs. F. L.	Tate St., Elberton, Ga.	50	50	50	50	360
2	Adams, Mrs. Parthenia J.	Bowman, Ga.	50				
3	Almond, Mrs. S. A. E.	Elberton, Ga. Added 1926	50	50	50	50	
4	Anderson, Mrs. Sara A.	Elberton, Ga., #8	50	50	50	50	260
5	Bond, Mrs. Nancy S.	Dewey Rose, Ga., #1	50	50	50	50	460
6	Booth, Mrs. L. C.	Dewey Rose, Ga., #1	50	50	50	50	260
7	Bowen, Mrs. Annie E.	Bowman, Ga.	50	50	50	50	260
8	Bowman, Mrs. A. E.	Middleton, Ga.	50	50	50	50	260
9	Brown, Mrs. Martha A.	Bowman, Ga.	50	50	50	50	260
10	Brown, Mrs. N. S.	Elberton, Ga.	50	50	50	50	260
11	Burch, Mrs. Ida J.	Elberton, Ga.	50	50	50	50	460
12	Burden, Mrs. S. C.	Dewey Rose, Ga. 16 Jul 1927	50	50	50	50	260

No.	Name	Address and Remarks	1st Qtr	2nd Qtr	3rd Qtr	4th Qtr	Past Due
13	Burriss, Mrs. Ann	Elberton, Ga., #8	50	50	50	50	260
14	Carpenter, Mrs. H. D.	Elberton, Ga., #6	50	50	50	50	260
15	Carpenter, Mrs. S. N.	S. Oliver St., Elberton, Ga. Added 4th Quarter 1926	50	50	50	50	260
16	Chandler, Mrs. L. E.	Thomas St. Elberton, Ga.	50	50	50	50	360
17	Charping, Mrs. S. E.	Elberton, Ga.	50	50	50	50	360
18	Cosby, Mrs. B. A.	Elberton, Ga.	50	50	50	50	260
19	Cox, Mrs. M. A.	Elberton, Ga.	50	50	50	50	260
20	Craft, Mrs. L. E.	Elberton, Ga.	50	50	50	50	260
21	Craft, Rosa C.	Elberton, Ga., #6	50	50	50	50	260
22	Dixon, Mrs. Mollie S.	Middleton, Ga., #1 Added 2nd Quarter 1926		50	50	50	
23	Fortson, Mrs. M. J.	340 Church St. Elberton, Ga.	50	50	50	50	460
24	Fortson, Mrs. S. B.	Elberton, Ga., #10 Died before Xmas 1925. $50 Returned.					
49	Stilwell, Mrs. Lillie Dora	Thomas St. Elberton, Ga.	50	50	50	50	60
50	Tate, Mrs. Mark Daniel	Justin St. Elberton, Ga. Died 4 Jan 1927	50	50	50	50	
51	Thornton, Mrs. Sallie C.	Elberton, Ga., #5	50	50	50	50	260

No.	Name	Address and Remarks	1st Qtr	2nd Qtr	3rd Qtr	4th Qtr	Past Due
52	Thornton, Mrs. S. E.	Elberton, Ga. Died before 1st Quarter Property	50				
53	Walker, Mrs. H. M.	Bowman, Ga.	50	50	50	50	460
54	Warren, Mrs. Antoinette	Elberton, Ga.	50	50	50	50	460
55	Webb, Mrs. Mary E.	Elberton, Ga., #5	50	50	50	50	360
56	Whitaker, Mrs. Mary	Bowman, Ga. Pd. Funeral Expenses $100 Miss Leona Haynes	50				
57	White, Mrs. L. M.	Elberton, Ga.	50	50	50	50	260
58	Whitman, Mrs. Elizabeth	Elberton, Ga.	50	50	50	50	260
59	Willis, Mrs. E. A.	Elberton, Ga.	50	50	50	50	460
60	Willis, Mrs. L. G.	R R St. Elberton, Ga.	50	50	50	50	360
	Dixon, Mrs. Laura A.	Abram Added 1st Quarter 1927					

1927 Widows Pension Roll

The following table presents the transcribed pension roll in six columns, the first column a consecutive number assigned to each widow, the second the name of the widow, the third her post office address, the fourth and fifth the pension amount paid the first two quarters of 1927, and the sixth all other information recorded by the clerk.

No.	Name	Address	1st Qtr	2nd Qtr	Remarks
25	Ginn, Mrs. Julia A.	Bowman, Ga.	50	50	
26	Ginn, Mrs. Mary	Bowman, Ga.	50	50	
27	Hewell, Mrs. S. A. C.	Dewey Rose, Ga.	50	50	
28	Hill, Mrs. Fannie	Elberton, Ga.	50	50	
29	Hilley, Mrs. S. E.	Elberton, Ga.	50	50	
30	Jones, Mrs. Miley A.	Elberton, Ga.	50	50	
31	Maxwell, Mrs. Amanda C.	Dewey Rose, Ga.	50	50	
32	Maxwell, Mrs. L. M.	Elberton, Ga.	50	50	
33	Maxwell, Mrs. Mary H.	Dewey Rose, Ga.	50	50	
34	Mauldin, Mrs. Permelia	Middleton, Ga.	50	50	
35	Moss, Mrs. Martha A.	Bowman, Ga.	50	50	
36	McLanahan, Mrs. T. C.	Elberton, Ga.	50	50	
37	McMullan, Mrs. J. L.	Elberton, Ga.	50	50	

No.	Name	Address	1st Qtr	2nd Qtr	Remarks
38	Norman, Mrs. M. J.	Dewey Rose, Ga.	50		Died 6 Apr 1927 Solvent
39	Rogers, Mrs. M. E.	Elberton, Ga.	50	50	
40	Seymour, Mrs. S.	Elberton, Ga.	50	50	
41	Smith, Mrs. Jennie	Elberton, Ga.	50	50	
42	Smith, Mrs. Mary Ann	Elberton, Ga.	50	50	
43	Snellings, Mrs. Frances	Elberton, Ga.	50	50	
44	Stilwell, Mrs. Lillie Dora	Elberton, Ga.	50	50	
45	Thornton, Sallie	Elberton, Ga.	50	50	
46	Walker, Mrs. H. M.	Bowman, Ga.	50	50	
47	Warren, Mrs. Antoinette	Elberton, Ga.	50	50	
48	Webb, Mrs. Mary E.	Elberton, Ga.	50	50	

1928 Widows Pension Roll

The following table presents the transcribed pension roll in five columns, the first column the name of the pensioner, the second, third, and fourth the pension amount paid the first three quarters of 1928, and the fifth all other information recorded by the clerk.

Name	1st Qtr	2nd Qtr	3rd Qtr	Remarks
Adams, Mrs. F. L.	50	50	50	
Anderson, Mrs. Sara A.	50	50	50	
Booth, Mrs. L. C.	50	50	50	
Bowman, Mrs. A. E.	50	50	50	
Brown, Mrs. Martha A.	50	50		Died 19 Apr 1928
Brown, Mrs. N. S.	50	50	50	
Burch, Mrs. Ida J.	50	50	50	
Carpenter, Mrs. H. D.				Died 21 Jan 1928 Solvent, no money sent down.
Carpenter, Mrs. S. N.	50	50	50	
Chandler, Mrs. L. E.	50	50	50	
Charping, Mrs. S. E.	50	50	50	
Cosby, Mrs. B. A.	50	50	50	
Craft, Mrs. Rosa C.	50	50	50	
Craft, Mrs. L. E.	50	50	50	
Dixon, Mrs. Mollie S.	50	50	50	
Fortson, Mrs. L. C.				Died 4 Oct 1927 Solvent, no money sent down.

Name	1st Qtr	2nd Qtr	3rd Qtr	Remarks
Fortson, Mrs. M. J.	50	50	50	
Galloway, Mrs. S. F.	50	50	50	
Ginn, Mrs. Julia A.	50	50	50	
Ginn, Mrs. Mary	50	50	50	
Hewell, Mrs. S. A. C.	50	50	50	
Hill, Mrs. Fannie	50	50	50	
Hilley, Mrs. S. E.	50	50	50	
Jones, Miley A.	50			Returned 14 Nov 1928 Dead
Sanders, Mrs. Ophelia		50	50	Added 31 May 1928. Husband, J. W. Sanders Co A, 1st Ga. Address, Bowman, Ga.

1921-1923 Widows Old Pension Roll

The following table presents the transcribed pension roll in six columns, the first column the name of the widow, the second her post office address, the third, fourth, and fifth the pension amount paid each year, and the six all other information recorded by the clerk.

Name	Address	1921	1922	1923	Remarks
Fortson, S. B.		125	100	100	
~~Fortson, Lucy J.~~	#5, Elberton, Ga				Died Dec 1920 Insolvent
Ginn, Julia A.	Bowman, Ga.	125	100	100	
Goss, Cora A.	#6, Elberton, Ga.	125	100	100	Died 30 May 1926
Galloway, S. F.	Elberton, Ga.	125	100	100	
~~Hairston, N. A.~~	~~Bowman, Ga.~~	100			Pd. to N. A. Hairston 24 Apr $25 returned Died 1921 Solvent
Hammond, Nancy F.	376 Long Ave. Elberton, Ga	125	100	100	
Hilley, Mary S. E	~~.#3, Elberton, Ga.~~ #1, Dewey Rose, Ga., c/o J. A. Hilley	125	100	100	
Hewell, S. A. C.	Dewey Rose, Ga.	125	100	100	
~~Higginbotham, Georgia~~	Elberton, Ga.	125			$100 Pd. to Mrs. Georgia Higginbotham, $25 Pd. Clark Edwards, Jr. and Died 16 Dec 1921 Insolvent

Name	Address	1921	1922	1923	Remarks
Jones, Miley A.	#1, Middleton, Ga.	125	100	100	
Moss, Martha A.	Bowman, Ga.	125	100	100	
Moon, A. S.	Bowman, Ga.	125			$100 Pd to Mrs. Moon $25 Pd to Clark Edwards, Jr. and Pd Funeral Expenses. Died 13 May 1921
Mattox, R. C.	Elberton, Ga.	125	100		Died 17 Mar 1921
Rousey, Malinda					

1920-1923 Widows New Pension Roll

The following table presents the transcribed pension roll in seven columns, the first column the year the widow was added to the pension roll, the second the name of the pensioner, the third her post office address, the fourth, fifth, and sixth the pension amount paid each year, and the seventh all other information recorded by the clerk.

When Added	Name	Address	1920	1921	1923	Remarks
1920	Auld, Rachel A.	Elberton, Ga.	100	125		Died 25 Feb 1922
1921	Adams, Mrs. F. R.	Elberton, Ga.		125	100	
1920	Bond, Nancy S.	Dewey Rose, Ga., #1	100	125		
1920	Booth, Mary E.	Elberton, Ga.				Died Sep 1921 Insolvent Sent to Insane Sanitarium in Sep 1920. $100 Returned. Struck from 1921 List.
1920	Burch, Ida J.	Elberton, Ga.	100	125		
1920	Cade, Laura B.		100	125		$225 Returned Died Solvent
1921	Chandler, L. E.	Elberton, Ga.		125	100	
1920	Cleveland, M. E.	c/o J. M. Cleveland Elberton, Ga.	100	125	100	
1920	Crawford, M. L.	Elberton, Ga., #6	100	125		Dead
1922	Charping, Mrs. S. E.	Elberton, Ga., #9			100	Husband W. L. Charping,

When Added	Name	Address	1920	1921	1923	Remarks
						Co H, 30 Ga
1920	Fortson, M. J.	Elberton, Ga.	100	125		
1921	Ginn, Mary	Bowman, Ga.		125	100	
~~1920~~	~~Hendrick, N. C.~~	Bowman, Ga.				Died 9 Apr 1922
~~1920~~	~~Higginbotham, Emma E.~~	Elberton, Ga., #2	100	125		
1923	Hill, Mrs. Fannie	Cancelled	100	125		Husband T. M. Hill Dead 12 Mar 1922 Solvent R. Higginbotham
1924	Harper, Mrs. Sara M.					
1921	Jones, M.	Elberton, Ga.		125	100	Dead
1920	Warren, Antoinette	Elberton, Ga., #2	100	125		
1902	Webb, Mary E.	Elberton, Ga., #5	100	125	100	
1920	Willis, L. G.	Elberton, Ga.	100	125	100	
1922	Willis, E. A.	Elberton, Ga., #6				Husband T. B. F. Willis Co C, 15 Ga

1924 Widows Pension Roll

The following table presents the transcribed pension roll in four columns, the first column the name of the pensioner, the second and third the pension amount paid in 1924, and the fourth all other information recorded by the clerk. Apparently, two separate payments were made during the year.

Name	1924	1924	Remarks
Adams, Mrs. F. L.	100	25	
Adams, Parthenia J.	100	25	Died 24 Mar 1926
Anderson, Sara A.	100	25	
Bond, Lucy C.	100		Pd. funeral expenses Died 7 Feb 1924
Bond, Nancy S.	100	25	
Booth, Mrs. L. C.	100	25	
Bowen, Annie E.	100	25	
Bowman, A. E.	100	25	
Brown, Martha A.	100	25	
Brown, N. S.	100	25	
Brown, S. C.		25	Returned. Died 1923
Brown, Winnie A.	100		Transferred to Madison County 31 Dec 1924
Burch, Ida J.	100	25	
Burden, S. C.	100	25	
Burriss, Ann	100	25	
Carpenter, H. D.	100	25	
Chandler, L. E.	100	25	

Name	1924	1924	Remarks
Charping, S. E.	100	25	
Clark, Sallie J.	100		Dead Aug 1924
Cleveland, M. E.	100	25	Died 15 Jan 1925
Cosby, B. A.	100	25	
Cox, M. A.	100	25	
Moss, Martha A.	100	25	
Maxwell, Amanda C.	100		Added 20 Oct 1925 Husband D. J. Maxwell
McCurry, Susan B.	100	25	Died 26 Mar 1926
McLanahan, T. C.	100	25	
McMullan, J. L.	100	25	1925
Nash, Rachel F.	100	25	Died 27 Dec 1925
Rogers, Mary E.	100	25	
Rousey, Malinda	100		Pd. funeral expenses. 19 Apr 1924
Sanders, Alpha	100		Pd. funeral expenses. 14 Apr 1924
Sanders, Mary A.	100	25	Died 29 May 1925
Seymour, S.	100	25	
Smith, Jenny	100	25	
Smith, Mattie A.	100	25	Died 1925
Smith, Nancy E.			Returned. Died 1925
Snellings, Frances L.	100	25	
Stilwell, Lillie Dora	100	25	Added 1 Jan 1925 Husband J. F. Stilwell

Name	1924	1924	Remarks
Thornton, Sallie C.	100	25	
Thornton, S. E.	100	25	Dead
~~Vickery, L. E.~~			Returned. Dead 1923
Walker, H. M.	100	25	

Undated Widows Pension Roll

The following table presents the transcribed pension roll in four columns, the first column the name of the pensioner, the second the name of her husband, the third the year she was added to the pension roll, and the fourth all other information recorded by the clerk. The pension roll apparently was compiled during the period 1926 through 1928, but does not record any pension payments.

Name	Husband	When Added	Remarks
Almond, Mrs. S. A. E.		1925 for 1926	Died May 1927
Tate, Mrs. Mark Daniel		1925 for 1926	
Maxwell, Mrs. Amanda C.	D. J. Maxwell	1925 for 1926	
Dixon, Mrs. Mollie S.	S. W. Dixon	1926 for 2nd Qtr	
Norman, Mrs. M. J.	E. B. Norman	1926 for 2nd Qtr	
Maxwell, Mrs. Mary H.	Chandler Maxwell	1926 for 2nd Qtr	
Smith, Mrs. Mary Ann	B. C. Smith Asst. Surgeon	1926 for 3rd Qtr	c/o Dr. A. C. Smith
Carpenter, Mrs. N. S.		1926 Oct 22 4th Qtr	
Dixon, Mrs. Laura A.	Abram Dixon	1927 Jan 26 1st Qtr	Died 20 Sep 1927
Fortson, Mrs. L. C.	A. C. Fortson	1927 Jul 26 3rd Qtr	Died 4 Oct 1927
Teasley, Mrs. Telitia Turner	J. A. Teasley	1928 Feb 3 1st Qtr	Died 1 Aug 1928
Snellings, Mrs. Frances			Died 7 Apr 1928
Slay, Mrs. Frances	G. F. Slay	30 Oct	

1925 Widows Pension Roll

The following table presents the transcribed pension roll in four columns, the first column the name of the pensioner, the second and third the pension amount paid in 1925, and the fourth all other information recorded by the clerk. Again apparently, two separate payments were made during the year.

Name	1925	1925	Remarks
Adams, Mrs. F. L.	100	40	
~~Adams, Catherine J.~~	100	40	Died 23 Mar 1926
Anderson, Sara A.	100	40	
Bond, Nancy S.	100	40	
Booth, Mrs. L. C.	100	40	
Bowen, Annie E.	100	40	
Bowman, A. E.	100	40	
Brown, Martha A.	100	40	
Brown, N. S.	100	40	
Burch, Ida J.	100	40	
Burden, S. C.	100	40	
Burris, Ann	100	40	
Carpenter, H. D.	100	40	
Chandler. L. E.	100	40	
Charping, S. E.	100	40	
Cosby, B. A.	100	40	
Cox, M. A.	100	40	
Craft, L. E.	100	40	

Name	1925	1925	Remarks
Craft, Rosa C.	100	40	
Cunningham, M. E.	100	40	Died 26 Nov 1925
Fortson, M. J.	100	40	
Fortson, S. R.	100	40	Dead
Galloway, S. F.	100	40	
Ginn, Julia A.	100	40	
Webb, Mary E	100	40	
Whitaker, Mary	100	40	
White, L. M.	100	40	
Whitman, Elizabeth	100	40	
Willis, E. A.	100	40	
Willis, L. G.	100	40	
Stillwell, Lillie Dora	100	40	
Cleveland, M. E.	100	40	
Carpenter, Mrs. N. S.			Added 22 Oct 1926 Died 15 Jan 1925

1926 Widows Pension Roll

The following table presents the transcribed pension roll in nine columns, a consecutive number assigned to each widow in the first column, the name of the widow in the second, and her post office address. The pension amounts paid for each quarter of 1926 are in the next four columns. The eighth column contains the total amount due each pensioner from previous years, but not yet paid. The last, or ninth, column contains all other information recorded by the clerk.

No.	Name	Address	1st Qtr	2nd Qtr	3rd Qtr	4th Qtr	Past Due	Remarks
25	Galloway, Mrs. S. F.	Elberton, Ga.	50	50	50	50	260	
26	Ginn, Mrs. Julia A.	Bowman, Ga.	50	50	50	50	260	
27	Ginn, Mrs. Mary	Bowman, Ga.	50	50	50	50	360	
28	Goss, Mrs. Cora A.	Elberton, Ga., #6	50					
29	Harper, Mrs. Sara M.	Elberton, Ga.						Died 22 Feb 1926
30	Hewell, Mrs. S. A. C.	Dewey Rose, Ga.	50	50	50	50	260	
31	Hill, Mrs. Fannie	Elberton, Ga.	50	50	50	50	310	
32	Hilley, Mrs. S. E.	Dewey Rose, Ga.	50	50	50	50	260	
33	Jones, Mrs. Miley A.	Elberton, Ga.	50	50	50	50	260	
34	Maxwell, Mrs. Amanda C.	Dewey Rose, Ga.	50	50	50	50		Added 1926 (1st)
35	Maxwell, Mrs. L. M.	Elberton, Ga.	50	50	50	50	460	
36	Maxwell, Mrs. Mary H.	Dewey Rose, Ga., #2		50	50	50		Added 1926 (2nd)

No.	Name	Address	1st Qtr	2nd Qtr	3rd Qtr	4th Qtr	Past Due	Remarks
37	Mauldin, Mrs. Permelia	Middleton, Ga.	50	50	50	50	460	
38	Moss, Mrs. Martha A.	Bowman, Ga.	50	50	50	50	260	
39	McCurry, Mrs. Susan B.	Elberton, Ga.	50					Died 26 Mar 1926 Property
40	McLanahan, Mrs. T. C.	Elberton, Ga.	50	50	50	50	360	
41	McMullan, Mrs. J. L.	Elberton, Ga., #9	50	50	50	50	310	
42	Nash, Mrs. Rachel F.	Elberton, Ga., #5						$50 Returned Died before Xmas 1925
43	Norman, Mrs. M. J.	Dewey Rose, Ga.		50	50	50		Added 1926 (2nd)
44	Rogers, Mrs. Mary E.	Thomas St. Elberton, Ga.	50	50	50	50	460	
45	Seymour, Mrs. S.	Elberton, Ga.	50	50	50	50	260	
46	Smith, Mrs. Jenny	S. Oliver St. Elberton, Ga.	50	50	50	50	260	
47	Smith, Mrs. Mary Ann	Elberton, Ga.			50	50		Added 3rd Quarter
48	Snellings, Mrs. Frances L.	Elberton, Ga.	50	50	50	50	260	

117

1927 Widows Pension Roll

The following table presents the transcribed pension roll in six columns, the first column a consecutive number assigned to each widow, the second the name of the widow, the third her post office address, the fourth and fifth the pension amount paid the first two quarters of 1927, and the sixth all other information recorded by the clerk.

No.	Name	Address	1st Qtr	2nd Qtr	Remarks
1	Adams, Mrs. F. L.	Elberton, Ga.	50	50	
2	Almond, Mrs. S. A. E.	Elberton, Ga.	50		Dead 7 May 1927 Refunded 21 May 1927
3	Anderson, Mrs. Sara A.	Elberton, Ga.	50	50	
4	Bond, Mrs. Nancy S.	Elberton, Ga.	50		Died 28 Mar 1927 Pd. $100 Funeral Expenses W. C. Allen
5	Booth, Mrs. L. C.	Dewey Rose, Ga.	50	50	
6	Bowen, Mrs. Annie E.	Bowman. Ga.	50	50	
7	Bowman, Mrs. A. E.	Middleton, Ga.	50	50	
8	Brown, Mrs. Martha A.	Bowman. Ga.	50	50	
9	Brown, Mrs. N. S.	Hartwell, Ga.	50	50	
10	Burch, Mrs. Ida J.	Elberton, Ga.	50	50	
11	Burden, Mrs. S. C.	Bowman. Ga.	50	50	Pd. M. E. Maxwell & Co $100 29 Aug 1927 Died 16 Jul 1927

No.	Name	Address	1st Qtr	2nd Qtr	Remarks
12	Burris, Mrs. Ann	Elberton, Ga.	50	50	
13	Carpenter, Mrs. H. D.	Elberton, Ga.	50	50	Died 21 Jan 1928
14	Carpenter, Mrs. S. N.	Elberton, Ga.	50	50	
15	Chandler, Mrs. L. E.	Elberton, Ga.	50	50	
16	Charping, Mrs. S. E.	Elberton, Ga.	50	50	
17	Cosby, Mrs. B. A.	Elberton, Ga.	50	50	
18	Cox, Mrs. M. A.	Elberton, Ga.	50	50	
19	Craft, Mrs. L. E.	Dewey Rose, Ga.	50	50	
20	Craft, Mrs. Rosa C.	Elberton, Ga.	50	50	
21	Dixon, Mrs. Laura A.	Elberton, Ga.	50	50	
22	Dixon, Mrs. Mollie S.	Middleton, Ga.	50	50	
23	Fortson, Mrs. N. J.	Elberton, Ga.	50	50	
24	Galloway, Mrs. S. F.	Barnesville, Ga.	50	50	
49	White, Mrs. L. M.	Elberton, Ga.	50	50	
50	Whitman, Elizabeth	Elberton, Ga.	50	50	
51	Willis, Mrs. E. A.	Elberton, Ga.	50	50	
52	Willis, Mrs. L. G.	Elberton, Ga.	50	50	
53	Roberts, Elizabeth J.	Bowman, Ga.		50	Husband W. C. Roberts, Co M, 25 Ga Added 20 May

119

No.	Name	Address	1st Qtr	2nd Qtr	Remarks
					1927
54	Fortson, Mrs. L. C.	c/o C. O. Hewell Elberton, Ga.			Husband Asa C. Fortson, Co H, 3 Ga Added Jul 1927 Pd. $50 4th Quarter c/o Transferee Died 4 Oct 1927
55	Tate, Mrs. Mark Daniel	Elberton, Ga.			Died 6 Jan 1927 Pd. $100 Funeral Expenses Murray Ins Co.

1928 Widows Pension Roll

The following table presents the transcribed pension roll in five columns, the first column the name of the pensioner, the second, third, and fourth the pension amount paid the first three quarters of 1928, and the fifth all other information recorded by the clerk.

Name	1st Qtr	2nd Qtr	3rd Qtr	Remarks
Maxwell, Amanda C.	50	50	50	
Maxwell, Mrs. L. M.	50	50	50	
Maxwell, Mrs. Mary H.	50	50	50	
Mauldin, Mrs. Permelia	50	50	50	
Moss, Mrs. Martha A.	50	50	50	
McLanahan, Mrs. T. C.	50	50	50	
McMullan, Mrs. J. L.	50	50	50	
Rogers, Mrs. Mary E.	50	50	50	
Roberts, Elizabeth J.	50	50	50	
Seymour, Mrs. S.	50	50	50	
Smith, Mrs. Jennie	50			Dead Solvent
Smith, Mrs. Mary Ann	50	50	50	
Snellings, Mrs. Frances L.				Returned 6 Jun 1928 Dead Insolvent
Stilwell, Lillie Dora	50	50	50	
Thornton, Sallie C.	50	50	50	
Walker, Mrs. H. M.	50	50	50	
Warren, Mrs. Antoinette	50	50	50	
Webb, Mrs. Mary E.	50			Returned 14 Nov 1928

121

Name	1st Qtr	2nd Qtr	3rd Qtr	Remarks
				Died 31 May 1928
White, Mrs. L. M.	50	50	50	
Whitman, Mrs. Elizabeth	50	50	50	
Willis, Mrs. E. A.	50	50	50	
Willis, Mrs. L. G.	50	50	50	
Teasley, Mrs. Telitia Turner	50	50		Returned 16 Nov 1928 Solvent Died 1928

1920-1922 Old Pension Roll

The following table presents the transcribed information in three columns, the first is the name of the pensioner, the second his post office address, and the third the pension amount paid and all other information recorded by the clerk.

Name	Address	Remarks
Brown, W. F.	Bowman, Ga.	$100 1921 Pd. to W. F. Brown $25 Returned, Died 1921 Solvent
Childs, S. G.	Elberton, Ga.	Changed to New List $115 Returned
Childs, S. G.	Elberton, Ga.	Added 1 Oct 1920 $90 1922

1927-1928 Pension Roll

The following table presents the transcribed information in five columns, the year the soldier was added to the pension roll in the first column, the name of the pensioner in the second, his disability in the third, and the pension amount paid in 1927 and 1928 in the last two columns.

When Added	Name	Disability	1927	1928
1927	Childs, S. G.	Loss of foot	40	40
1927	Hudson, W. A. C.	Loss of sight	90	90
1929	Gulley, Jno.	Loss of sight		

Deaths and Transfers on Old List & New List

On the last page of the original volume, the clerk recorded three deaths, as follows.

Mrs. Georgia Higginbotham (Widow) died Dec-5-1921.   Insolvent.   Husband (Robert Higginbotham) (Old List) 12/16/21

J. L. McMullan (Soldier) died Nov-11-1921.   Left Widow (Mrs. Judy Ann McMullan)   (New List) 12/16/21

Mrs. L. J. Thornton (Widow) died Dec-15-1921.   Solvent.   Husband (Wm. Thornton)   (New List) 12/16/21

Volume IV

On the outside front cover of the original volume, the clerk wrote *Pension Roll of Elbert County.* The original volume begins with a series of Pension Statements, printed forms recording the total number of pensioners in various categories and the total amounts paid to them by category for the years 1909 through 1916. The remaining records consists of pension rolls, lists of resident soldiers and widows living in 1923, a certificate documenting one widow's pension record before transferring to Elbert County, and a list of pensioners who were owed late pension payments.

Pension Statements

The pension statements are separate preprinted slips of paper, perhaps receipts, apparently pasted or otherwise affixed to the first pages of the original volume recording the total number of pensioners in various categories as well as the total amounts paid, by category, to the county for disbursement to the pensioners for the years 1909 through 1916. From year to year the different categories changed. The County Ordinary, L. C. Edwards, signed all of the receipts. The category titled *Pink Widows* evidently indicated widows who were solvent and healthy as opposed to *Indigent Widows*. The careful observer will notice that the total number of pensioners and the total amounts paid to them do not tally with the numbers above them, due primarily with the faint images on the microfilm.

	1909		1910		1911		1912	
	No.	Total	No.	Total	No.	Total	No.	Total
Indigent Soldiers	103	$6180	100	$6000	87	$5575	81	$4860
Indigent Widows	26	$1560	28	$10800	25	$1480	23 25	$1500
Pink Widows	19	$1140	19	$11400	17	$1020	17 16	$960
Disabled Soldiers	21	$1300	26	$12050	19	$1160	10	$900
1910 Widows	--	--	--	--	14	$800	24	$1440
1910 Soldiers	--	--	--	--	--	--	9	$540
Total	169	$10180	167	$14025	168	$10035	171	$10200
Signed	9 Jan 1909		8 Jan 1910		7 Jan 1911		8 Jan 1912	

	1913		1914	
	No.	Total	No.	Total
Indigent Soldiers	68	$4080	56	$3360
Indigent Widows	21	$1260	19	$1140
Pink Widows	13	$780	12	$720
Disabled Soldiers	10	$525	8	$425
1910 Soldiers	14	$840	18	$1080
1910 Widows	25	$1500	34	$2040
Total	151	$8885	147	$8765
Signed	4 Jan 1913		7 Jan 1914	

	1915		1916	
	No.	Total	No.	Total
All Widows	63	$3780	63*	[torn]
Indigent and Service Soldiers	72	$4320	70	[torn]
Disabled Soldiers	7	$400	7	[torn]
Total	142	$8500	141	[torn]
Signed	9 Jan 1915		10 Jan 1916	

*1 w/ Sarah Oglesby

Disabled or Invalid Soldiers Roll

While undated, the disabled or invalid soldiers roll essentially is a list of those veterans who qualified for a pension based upon their disability. The following table presents the transcribed information in five columns. The first column includes the name of the pensioner, the second and third column contain his company and regiment or other unit in which he served, the forth column includes a description of his disability, and the fifth column includes the names of the men who witnessed his pension application.

Name	Co	Regiment	Disability	Witnesses
Anderson, J. Eli	F		Lost leg at 2nd Manassas 30 Aug 1862	Geo. L. Almond Jasper Bryan, MD
Anderson, J. H.	D		Disabled by disease	A. E. Hammond N. G. Long, MD
Brown, W. F.	B	24	Enlisted Aug 1861 Arm Wound	Geo. T. Cauthen S. M. Bobo
Brown, J. W.				
Bagwell, M. V.	C	8	Lost finger at Wilderness, Virginia 6 May 1864	A. L. Johnson, MD F. E. Harper, MD Geo. L. Almond
Bond, E. M.	H	30	Lost toe at 2 Manassas 28 May 1862	B. F. Smith, MD H. B. Harper, MD G. D. Thornton
Booth, J. W.	F	38	Lost leg at Fishers Hill, Virginia 24 Sep 1864	Geo. L. Almond
Brown, B. W.	F	38	Disabled arm at Fredericksburg 13 Dec 1862	Geo. L. Almond
Brown, E. W.	F	38	Lost 2 fingers at Gettysburg 1863	Geo. L. Almond J. B. Bell, MD L. P. Eberhard, MD
Bond, E. M.	H	38	Disabled useless leg at	W. Culliam

Name	Co	Regiment	Disability	Witnesses
			Manassas 30 Aug 1862	B. F. Smith, MD
Bailey, F. D.	F	15	Useless arm	J. A. Johnson, MD T. D. Hunt L. L. Ware, MD
Balchin, Thos. P.	F	15	Body hurt, rupture	D. B. Vardell, MD J. J. Burch, Sr.
Balmon, J. W.	G	2 SC	Lost left leg near Richmond, Virginia 7 Oct 1864	Geo. L. Almond A. L. J. Stovall, MD
Booth, Absalom	H	38	Left leg disabled at Richmond, Virginia 29 Jun 1862	N. G. Long, MD Geo. L. Almond
Berger, C. L.	C	44	Transferred from Clarke Transferred to Clarke County 5 Jan 1906	

Ex-Confederate Soldiers Living in Elbert County, January 1, 1923

The pre-printed form is titled *List of Ex-Confederate Soldiers Living in this, Elbert, County, January 1, 1923*. The following table presents the transcribed information in five columns. The first column includes the name of the soldier, the second and third columns include the company and regiment or other unit in which the soldier served, the fourth column includes the date and place where the soldier enlisted, and the fifth column includes the date and place where the soldier was surrendered or discharged.

Name	Co	Regiment	Enlisted	Discharged
Adams, John D.	I	15 Ga	1861 Elberton, Ga	1865 Appomattox, Virginia
Allmond, Jesse M.	C	7 Ga Cavalry	1863 Savannah, Ga	1865 Augusta, Ga.
Adams, Hiram G.	H	38 Ga	1861 Elberton, Ga.	1864 Point Lookout, Maryland
Adams, L. M.				1865
Adams, Tinsley R.	F	38 Ga	1863 Elberton, Ga.	1865 Point Lookout, Maryland
Anderson, J. E.	F	Holcomb's Legion	1862 [faint] River, SC	1865 Donaldson[torn]
Adams, William M.	G	37 Ga	1862 Elberton, Ga.	1865 Augusta, Ga.
Anderson, William G.	I	15 Ga	1861 Elberton, Ga.	1865 Appomattox, Virginia
Adams, S. A.	M	9 Ga Battalion	1863 Elberton, Ga.	1865 Macon, Ga.
Adams, J. W.	H	3 Ga State Troops	1863 Elberton, Ga.	1865 Atlanta, Ga.
Almond, I. B.	F	38 Ga	1861 Elberton, Ga.	Ft. D[torn]
Adams, M. B.	D	9 Ga Battalion	1861 Elberton, Ga.	1865 Appomattox, Virginia

Name	Co	Regiment	Enlisted	Discharged
Andrews, A. J.	A	15 Ga	1862 Delphi, Ga.	1864 at home
Adams, R. E.	D	9 Ga	1862 Elberton, Ga.	1865 Augusta, Ga.
Adams, W. H. H.	H	State Troops	1862 Elberton, Ga.	1865 Augusta, Ga.
Arnold, McAlpin	D	1 Ga Reserves	1862 Elberton, Ga.	1865 at home
Bond, Andrew J.	F	38 Ga	1862 Fort Tawny Isles	1865 Appomattox, Virginia
Bond, James W.	H	38 Ga	1862 Savannah, Ga.	1865 Appomattox, Virginia
Booth, John W.	H	38 Ga	1862 Savannah, Ga.	1864 Fishers Hill, Virginia
Brown, James M.	H	38 Ga	1864 Elberton, Ga.	1865 at home
Bailey, E. P.	G	37 Ga	1862 Elberton, Ga.	1865 Greensborough, North Carolina
Brown, John D.	H	38 Ga	1861 Savannah, Ga.	1865 Appomattox, Virginia
Bartlett, William	I	14 SC	1861 [faint] South Carolina	1865 H. Island, Ky.
Barton, David F.				
Brown, B. T	F	38 Ga	1861 Elberton, Ga.	1865 Elbert County
Brown, Ben D.	C	7 Ga Cavalry	1863 Elberton, Ga.	1865 Greensborough, North Carolina
Burch, J. J.	F	15 Ga	1861 Elberton, Ga.	1865 Appomattox, Virginia
Bond, E. M.	H	3 Ga	1861 Elberton, Ga.	1865 Atlanta, Ga.
Brown, J. R.	B	24 Ga	1861 Hartwell, Ga.	1865 Appomattox,

Name	Co	Regiment	Enlisted	Discharged
				Virginia
Beasley, John		SC Home Guards		
Bell, George S.	C	15 Ga	1862 Elberton, Ga.	1865 Elberton, Ga.
Butler, Thomas N.	H	38 Ga	1861 Elberton, Ga.	1865 Point Lookout, Maryland
Biggs, Thomas D.	I	15 Ga	1861 Elberton, Ga.	1865 Augusta, Ga.
Bailey, N. L.	G	37 Ga	1862 Elberton, Ga.	1865 Greensborough, North Carolina
Brown, W. F.	B	34 Ga	1861 Eagle Grove Hart Av	1865 Appomattox, Virginia
Burriss, Joseph N.	H	24 SC	1864 Anderson, South Carolina	1865 Camp Douglass
Brownlee, J. W.		Beauregard Artillery	1863	1865
Brewer, John M.	C	7 Ga Cavalry	1862 Savannah, Ga.	1865 Appomattox, Virginia
Bailey, L. L.	G	37 Ga	1862 Elberton	1865 Greensborough, North Carolina
Bagwell, M. V.	C	16 Ga	1863 Hartwell, Ga.	1865 Appomattox, Virginia
Childs, J. B.	G	34 Ga	1861 Carnesville, Ga.	1865 Jonesborough
Charpin, Willis L.	H	30 Ga	1865 Atlanta, Ga.	1865 Augusta, Ga.
Cosby, N. B., Sr.	C	15 Ga	1861 Elberton, Ga.	1865 Appomattox, Virginia
Baron, D. P.	I	2 SC Artillery	1861	1865 Sullivan Isl.

133

Name	Co	Regiment	Enlisted	Discharged
Colwell, A. V.	C	15 Ga	1862 Elberton, Ga.	1865 Appomattox, Virginia
Cox, W. C.	I	16 Ga	1861 Louisville, Ga.	1865 Appomattox, Virginia
Cleveland, R. W.	I	15 Ga	1861 Elberton, Ga.	1865 Appomattox, Virginia
Craft, Wm. A.	F	15 Ga	1862 Elberton, Ga.	1865 Appomattox, Virginia
Crawford, Francis M.	M	Lee's Bat	1864 Atlanta, Ga.	1865 Macon, Ga.
Colvard, H. H.	F	39 NC	1861 Murphy Bor., North Carolina	1865 Fort Delaware, Maryland
Cleveland, D. E.	I	15 Ga	1861 Elberton, Ga.	1865 Rock Island
Cosby, D. C.	C	15 Ga	1861 Elberton, Ga.	1865 Appomattox, Virginia
Campbell, J. E.	H	38 Ga	1862 Elberton, Ga.	1865 Appomattox, Virginia
Bailey, F. O.	F	15 Ga	1861 Elberton, Ga.	1865 Appomattox, Virginia
Burden, J. J.	D	37 Ga.	1862 Elberton, Ga.	1865 Augusta, Ga.
Daniel, R. L.	K	2 Ga	1862 Elberton, Ga.	1865
Colvard, J. E.	H	38 Ga	1862 Elberton, Ga.	1865 Appomattox, Virginia
Dixon, S. W.	C	7 Ga Cavalry	1863 Isle of Hope	1865 Point Lookout, Maryland
Davis, Wm. P.	C	2 SC	1861 Pickens Dist.	1865 Pickens Dist., South Carolina
Dixon, Andrew W.	C	7 Ga Cavalry		

Name	Co	Regiment	Enlisted	Discharged
Eavenson, Willis J.	F	38 Ga	1861 Goss, Ga.	1865 Madison, Ga.
Elgin, W. D.	B	4 SC Bat	1864 Abbeville, South Carolina	1865 Greenville, South Carolina
[torn]son, John W.	F	38 Ga	1861 Elberton, Ga.	1865 Macon, Ga.
[torn] J. A.	H	15 Ga	1861 Elberton	1865 Horns on Furland
[torn]nney, J. H.	H	3 Ga State Troops	1864 Macon, Ga.	1865 Fort Delaware, Maryland
[torn]ning, Laurence	D	1 Ga Reserves	1864 Elberton, Ga.	1865 Albany, Ga.
[torn]tson, George H.	I	7 Ga Cavalry	1863 Elberton, Ga.	1865 Elberton, Ga.
[torn]tson, E. R.	I	15 Ga	1861 Elberton, Ga.	1865 Appomattox, Virginia
[torn]tson, John B.	I	15 Ga	1862 Elberton, Ga.	1865 Appomattox, Virginia
Fortson, D. A.	I	15 Ga	1862 Elberton, Ga.	1865 Appomattox, Virginia
Fortson, Wm. E.	I	15 Ga	1861 Elberton, Ga.	1865 Appomattox, Virginia
Fortson, M. E.	I	15 Ga	1861 Elberton, Ga.	1865 Appomattox, Virginia
Fleming, E. B.	C	15 Ga	1864 Hartwell, Ga.	1865 Augusta, Ga.
Gaines, R. A.		7 Ga Cavalry	1862 Savannah, Ga.	1865 Appomattox, Virginia
Glower, J. D.	F	15 Ga	1861 Elberton, Ga.	1865 Appomattox, Virginia
Ginn, T. J.	K	2 Ga	1863 Elberton, Ga.	1865 Rock, Ga.

Name	Co	Regiment	Enlisted	Discharged
Ginn, Gaines W.	H	38 Ga	1861 Elberton, Ga.	1865 Spotsylvania, Virginia
Ginn, I. L.		7 Ga Cavalry	1863 Savannah, Ga.	1865 Home on Detail
Galloway, R. B.	F	15 Ga	1861 Elberton, Ga.	1865 Appomattox, Virginia
Guest, B. D.	G	2 SC Rifles	1862 Anderson, South Carolina	1865 Appomattox, Virginia
Hudson, W. A. C.	C	7 Ga Cavalry	1863 Elberton, Ga.	1865 Point Lookout, Maryland
[torn]ins, J. D.	F	15 Ga	1861 Elberton, Ga.	1865 Appomattox, Virginia

1896-1909 Indigent Soldiers Pension Roll

The following table presents the transcribed information in six columns. The first column includes the name of the soldier, the second and third columns include the company and regiment or other unit in which the soldier served, the fourth column includes the justification for granting the pension, the fifth column includes the names of the men who witnessed the pension application, and the sixth column includes the date of enlistment, date and place of discharge or surrender, and the pension amounts paid and year of payment. Occasionally, the clerk recorded certain information in the wrong column.

Name	Co	Regiment	Cause of Pension	Witnesses	Service & Amount Paid
Smith, Luther G.		Norman's Company Toombs' Brigade	Infirmity & poverty	N. L. Long, MD A. J. Mathews, MD A. E. Mathews, MD	1863 until mustered out, served 8 or 10 months $60 1896-1897, new application, $60 1904, transferred Oglethorpe
Snellings, W. H.	C	7 Ga Cavalry	Infirmity & poverty		1862 $60 1905, 1909
Smith, Jas. W.	A	1 Ga	Infirmity & poverty	Transferred to Wilkes County 1908	1863 $60 1905
Smith, W. T.	C	15 Ga		N. S. Cosby J. E. Johnson	1863 until surrendered at Appomattox, Virginia 9 Apr 1865 $60 1909
Snellings, G. W.	C	15 Ga	Age & poverty	A. V. Caldwell A. Webb F. O. Bailey	1861 to 9 Apr 1865 $60 1905, 1909

Name	Co	Regiment	Cause of Pension	Witnesses	Service & Amount Paid
Snellings, G. T.	C	7 Ga Cavalry	Age & poverty	J. M. Brown A. L. J. Stovall	1862 to 9 Apr 1865 $60 1905, 1909
Scoggins, J. W.		Echols' Artillery	Infirmity & poverty	T. A. Adams O. A. Walker, MD	1862 and served until at home on furlough at time of surrender $60 1905, 1909
Smith, J. Willis	C	15 Ga	Age & poverty	E. B. Tate	1861 to Apr 1865 $60 1909
Sanders, W. A.	B	23 Ga	Infirmity & poverty	C. C. Tislin M. C. Atkins Arnold	Jul 1863 to Apr 1864 $60 1909
Treadwell, Perry	I	15 Ga	Age & poverty	A. L. J. Stovall, MD J. E. Johnson, MD H. W. Snellings	1861 to close of war $60 1896
Terry, Jno. W.	F	15 Ga	Age & poverty	N. G. Long. MD J. E. Johnson, MD D. B. Alexander	1862 to 1863 $60 1896-1898
Thomason, H. H.	K	2 Ga State Troops	Age & poverty	C. E. Earle, MD A. J. Mathews, MD B. E. Daniel	1862 to close of war $60 1896, 1897
Terrell, J. B.	K	2 Ga	Age & poverty	A. J. Mathews, MD D. B. Hunt	1862 to close of war $60 1898-1905, 1909
Thornton, M. J.	I	15 Ga	Age & poverty	B. F. Smith, MD A. S. Oliver, MD J. L. Deadwyler	1861 to capture 1864 $60 1904, 1905, 1909

Name	Co	Regiment	Cause of Pension	Witnesses	Service & Amount Paid
Turner, Jno. W.	G	37 Ga	Age & poverty	N. G. Long, MD A. L. J. Stovall, MD E. T. Bailey	1862 to close of war $60 1904 Dead
Thornton, W. E.	H	Toombs'	Age & poverty		Served 6 months $60 1905, 1909
Tate, J. B.	C	15 Ga	Age & poverty	J. E. Johnson E. R. Fortson	1861 to 9 Apr 1865 $60 1905, 1909
Thornton, J. C.	C	7 Ga Cavalry	Age & poverty	J. M. Almond	1863 $60 1909
Wansley, Thos. M.	F	38 Ga	Infirmity, age, & poverty	J. E. Cole, MD C. E. Clark, MD E. B. Higginbotham	1862 to close of war $60 1896-1904, 1909
Willis, J. S.	A	Harker's Battery	Age & poverty	J. E. Johnson, MD A. L. J. Stovall, MD J. M. Brewer	1862 to close of war $60 1897-1904, 1909
Wheeler, D. M.	C	15 Ga	Age & poverty	C. E. Clark, MD A. J. Mathews, MD R. W. Willis	1861, during war. $60 1899-1902
White, T. R.	I	15 Ga	Infirmity & poverty	J. B. Bell, MD A. J. Mathews, MD J. L. Deadwyler	1861 to close of war $60 1902-1904
Warren, D. H.	H	Toombs' Brigade	Infirmity & poverty	C. E. Clark, MD A. J. Mathews, MD B. E. Adams	1863 until disbanded, served 6 months $60 1903-1904, 1909

Name	Co	Regiment	Cause of Pension	Witnesses	Service & Amount Paid
White, A. L.	F	15 Ga	Age & poverty	J. S. Christian, MD B. W. Hall, MD D. B. Alexander	1861 and served until captured at Gettysburg Jul 1863. $60 1903-1904, 1909
Willis, T. B. F.	C	15 Ga	Age & poverty	A. S. Oliver, MD C. E. Clark, MD J. L. Deadwyler	1861 and served until captured at Gettysburg Jul 1863 $60 1903-1904, 1909
Webb, A. J.	I	38 Ga	24 Dec 1905	A. C. Holliday B. B. Mattox	1861 $60 1909
Young, J. C.	A	3 Ga	Infirmity & poverty	J. E. Johnson, MD A. J. Mathews, MD T. J. Herndon	1863 to close of war. $60 1896-1904, 1909
Letter "B" brought forward					
Brown, B. D.	C	7 Ga Cavalry	Infirmity & poverty	Thos. A. Jones	Aug 1863, on 24 Dec 1864 detailed for separate duty to surrender. $60 1909
Beasley, J. J.	G	1 SC State Troops	Age & poverty	Thos. M. Hill	Sep 1864 to 20 Apr 1865 at Spartanburg, South Carolina. Died 1908
Brown, John S.	G	37 Ga		A. R. Holderby, MD E. Griffin, MD	Mar 1862 Transferred from Madison County 10 Dec

Name	Co	Regiment	Cause of Pension	Witnesses	Service & Amount Paid
				D. P. Oglesby	1907 Died 1908
Burden, J. W.	D	11 Ga Cavalry			Transferred from Wilkes County. 1865 1 Nov 1909
Letter "C" brought forward					
Chambers, J. C.	B	55 Ga	Indigent	G. C. Brewer N. L. Aron, MD	Jun 1862 to May 1865 Camp Douglas. Transferred from Oglethorpe County 18 Nov 1908. $60 1909
Cleveland, R. W.	I	15 Ga	Infirmity & poverty	N. B. Cosby	Jun 1861 to Apr 1865 surrender. $60 1909

1909-1920 Indigent Soldiers Pension Roll

The following table presents the transcribed information in six columns. The first column includes the name of the soldier, the second and third columns include the company and regiment or other unit in which the soldier served, the fourth column includes the justification for granting the pension, the fifth column includes the names of the men who witnessed the pension application, and the sixth column includes the pension amounts paid and year of payment.

Name	Co	Regiment	Cause	Witnesses	Amount Paid
Adams, L. M.					$60 1909-1916 $70 1917 $80 1918 Died 31 Mar 1918.
Andrew, A. J.					$60 1909-1914 Died 21 Dec 1914. Widow
Anderson, W. G.					$60 1909-1914 Died 20 Feb 1914.
Adams, J. D.					$60 1909-1915 3 Jul 1915
Almond, J. M.					$60 1909-1912 Died 25 Dec 1912.
Brown, J. M.					$60 1909-1916 $70 1917 $80 1918 $90 1919 $100 1920
Biggs, T. D.					$60 1909-1910 Transferred to Wilkes County 5 Nov 1910.
Bell, G. S.					$60 1909-1916

Name	Co	Regiment	Cause	Witnesses	Amount Paid
					$70 1917 $80 1918 $90 1919 $100 1920
Brownlee, J. W.					$60 1909-1913 Died 2 Apr 1913.
Bailey, W. L.					$60 1909-1911 Died 3 Nov 1911
Braugh, W. H.					$60 1909-1916 $70 1917 $80 1918 $90 1919 Died 18 Jun 1919.
Bond, J. W.					$60 1909-1910 Died 7 Mar 1910.
Bradford, J. M.					$60 1909-1912 Died 5 Dec 1912.
Broadwell, J. M.					$60 1909 Died 12 Apr 1909.
Burden, J. J.					$60 1909-1911 Died 28 Dec 1911.
Bagwell, M. V.					$60 1909-1910 Died 8 Nov 1910.
Brewer, J. M.					$60 1909-1910 Died 22 May 1910.
Bailey, L. L.					$60 1909-1916

Name	Co	Regiment	Cause	Witnesses	Amount Paid
					$70 1917 $80 1918 $90 1919 $100 1920
Bailey, E. P.					$60 1909-1910 Died 31 Oct 1910.
Brown, B. D.					$60 1909-1916 $70 1917 $80 1918 $90 1919 $100 1920
Burden, J. W.	D	11 Ga Cavalry		N. J. Gumble R. Coner	Transferred from Wilkes County 1 Nov 1909. Transferred to Wilkes County 30 Dec 1911. Transferred from Wilkes County 9 Dec 1912. $60 1910, 1911, 1913 Died 5 Sep 1913.
Cosby, N. B.					$60 1909-1913 Died 24 May 1913.
Cosby, D. C.					$60 1909-1913 Transferred to Richmond County 22 Jul 1913.
Christian, J. W.					$60 1909 Died 1909.

Name	Co	Regiment	Cause	Witnesses	Amount Paid
Cox, J. H.					$60 1909-1913 Died 12 Jun 1913.
Craft, J. M.					$60 1909-1913 Died 22 Jul 1913.
Cox, W. C.					$60 1909-1910 Died 4 May 1910.
Conwell, J. O.					$60 1909-1916 $70 1917 $80 1918 $90 1919 $100 1920
Craft, W. A.					$60 1909-1910 Died 20 Apr 1910.
Chambers, J. C.					$60 1909-1912 Died 10 Dec 1912.
Cleveland, R. W.					$60 1909-1916 $70 1917 $80 1918 $90 1919 $100 1920
Chaffen, John C.	E	38 Ga		W. W. Rosewell R. P. Service	Transferred from Fulton County 23 Dec 1913. $60 1914 Sep 1914
Dixon, A. W.					$60 1909-1916 $70 1917 $80 1918 $90 1919 $100 1920

145

Name	Co	Regiment	Cause	Witnesses	Amount Paid
Dickerson, C. Y.					$60 1909-1913 Died 1913.
Dixon, S. W.					$60 1909-1916 $70 1917 $80 1918 $90 1919 $100 1920
Daniel, R. L.					$60 1909-1912 Died 14 Jun 1912.
Davis, W. P.					$60 1909-1916 $70 1917 $80 1918 $90 1919 $100 1920
Dixon, Abram					$60 1909-1916 $70 1917 $80 1918 $90 1919 $100 1920
Eaverson, J. W.					$60 1909-1916 $70 1917 $80 1918 $90 1919 $100 1920
Eaton, W. A.		34 Ga		C. W. Oran J. D. Daniel, MD	Transferred from Madison County 26 Aug 1916. $70 1917 $80 1918 $90 1919 Returned for 1920.
Frost, W. T.					$60 1909-1912 Died 24 May 1912.

Name	Co	Regiment	Cause	Witnesses	Amount Paid
Fortson, W. E.					$60 1909-1916 $70 1917 $80 1918 $90 1919 Died 13 Aug 1919.
Field, W. G.					$60 1909-1910 Died 1 Sep 1910.
Fortson, M. E.					$60 1909-1916 $70 1917 $80 1918 $90 1919 Died 12 Mar 1919.
Fleming, J. H.					$60 1909-1916 $70 1917 $80 1918 $90 1919 $100 1920
Gully, A. Y.					$60 1909 Dead 1909.
Galloway, Richard					$60 1909 Died 29 Dec 1909.
Guest, S. B.					$60 1909-1916 $70 1917 $80 1918 $90 1919 $100 1920
Gully, J. W.					$60 1909-1916 $70 1917 $80 1918 $90 1919 $100 1920
Hill, T. M.					$60 1909-1916 $70 1917

Name	Co	Regiment	Cause	Witnesses	Amount Paid
					$80 1918 $90 1919 $100 1920
Hunt, S. J. W.					$60 1909-1914 Died Apr 1914.
Higginbotham, J. H.					$60 1909-1916 $70 1917 $80 1918 $90 1919 $100 1920
Hamilton, H. F.					$60 1909-1916 Died 3 Feb 1916.
Hilley, J. M.					$60 1909-1916 $70 1917 $80 1918 $90 1919 Died 29 Jan 1919.
Harper, Virgil E.					$60 1909-1911 Died 21 Apr 1911.
Hall, A. O.					$60 1909-1916 $70 1917 $80 1918 $90 1919 $100 1920
Hester, T. J.					$60 1909 Dead 1909.
Hammond, J. L.					$60 1909-1913 Transferred to Madison County 28 Feb 1913.
Hewell, Thos. J.					$60 1909-1916 $70 1917

Name	Co	Regiment	Cause	Witnesses	Amount Paid
					$80 1918 Died 19 Dec 1918.
Higginbotham, R. G.					Approved 1911 died 5 Mar 1918. $60 1912-1916 $70 1917 $80 1918

1909-1920 Disabled or Injured Soldiers Roll

The following table presents the transcribed information in six columns. The first column includes the name of the soldier, the second and third columns include the company and regiment or other unit in which the soldier served, the fourth column includes a description of the soldier's disability, the fifth column includes the names of the men who witnessed the pension application, and the sixth column includes the pension amounts paid and year of payment and all other information recorded by the clerk.

Name	Co	Regiment	Disability	Witnesses	Amount Paid and Remarks
Anderson, J. E.					$100 1909-1911 Died 30 May 1911.
Bond, E. M.					$50 1909-1914 Died 2 Oct 1914.
Booth, J. W.					$100 1909-1916 Died 21 May 1916.
Brown, B. T.					$50 1909-1912 Died 6 Sep 1912.
Bailey, F. O.					$50 1909-1912 Transferred to 1910 List. 1913
Burger, C. L.					$50 1909 Transferred to Wash 15 Dec 1909.
Brown, W. F.					$50 1909-1916 $60 1917 $70 1918 $80 1919

Name	Co	Regiment	Disability	Witnesses	Amount Paid and Remarks
					$90 1920
Campbell, J. E.					$50 1909-1916 $60 1917 $70 1918 $80 1919 Died 9 Jun 1919.
Colvard, John W.					$5 1909-1912 $25 1913-1914 Transferred to $25.00. 1913 Died 18 May 1914.
Childs, S. G.					Transferred from Franklin County 23 Dec 1916. $60 1917 $70 1918 $80 1919 $90 1920
Gaines, T. S.					$50 1909-1912 Died 9 Aug 1912.
Ginn, G. W.					$50 1909-1916 $60 1917 Died 1 May 1917.
Ginn, Tinsley J.					$50 1909-1912 Died 7 Nov 1912.
Hammond, A. E.					$50 1909-1910 Died 17 Dec 1909.

Name	Co	Regiment	Disability	Witnesses	Amount Paid and Remarks
Heard, R. M.					$50 1909-1910 Died Jan 1910.
Higginbotham, E. B.					$50 1909-1912 Died 20 Jun 1912.
Hill, J. M.					$50 1909-1911 Died
Mann, E. J.					Dec 1909
Oglesby, William					Transferred 1910 Roll 1914.
Saxon, L. W.					Died 3 Nov 1911.
Thornton, J. C.					Died 22 Nov 1917.
Vickery, W. J.					Died 16 Dec 1912.
Wood, Wiley	F	18 Ga		J. W. Wood J. M. Wood Joel M. Denen	Served 1862 to 1865. Transferred from Clarke. Transferred to 1910, for 1913.
Webb, M. D.	D	15 Ga		A. J. Webb N. M. Mattox T. A. Moon	Served Jul 1861 to Appomattox Apr 1865.

1896-1909 Indigent Soldiers Pension Roll

The following table presents the transcribed information in six columns. The first column includes the name of the soldier, the second and third columns include the company and regiment or other unit in which the soldier served, the fourth column includes the justification for granting the pension, the fifth column includes the names of the men who witnessed the pension application, and the sixth column includes the date of enlistment, date and place of discharge or surrender, and the pension amounts paid and year of payment.

Name	Co	Regiment	Cause	Witnesses	Service and Amount Paid
Anderson, S. T.	H	12 Ga	Infirmity & poverty	A. L. J. Stovall, MD A. J. Mathews, MD J. L. Saxon	1863 and served until captured Mar 1865. $60 1900-1905 Dead
Adams, L. M.	H	Toombs Brigade	Infirmity & poverty	A. J. Mathews, MD A. C. Mathews, MD R. E. Adams	1863 and served until disbanded 1864. $60 1903-1905, 1909
Andrews, A. J.	A	15 Ga	Age & poverty		Served 3 years. $60 1904-1905, 1909
Ashworth, Joel J.	H	19 SC	Age & poverty	N. G. Long, MD A. J. Mathews, MD A. M. Shumate	1864 and served to close of war. $60 1896-1897 Dead
Adams, R. C.	I	15 Ga	Age & poverty	N. G. Long, MD J. E. Johnson, MD W. H. Holme	1861 $60 1896
Alexander, D. B.	F	15 Ga	Age & infirmity	Served before paid	1861

Name	Co	Regiment	Cause	Witnesses	Service and Amount Paid
Anderson, W. G.	I	15 Ga	Age & poverty		1861 $60 1905, 1909
Adams, J. D.	I	15	Infirmity & poverty	E. R. Fortson	1861 $60 1909
Almond, J. M.	C	7 Ga Cavalry	Age & poverty	J. C. Thornton	1863 $60 1909
Brown, J. M.	H	38 Ga	Infirmity & poverty	J. E. Campbell A. J. Mathews	1864 $60 1905,1909
Biggs, T. D.	I	15 Ga	Age & poverty	M. J. Thornton J. E. Johnson, MD N. G. Long, MD	1861 to discharge. Substitute. Served 8 months. $60 1909
Bell, G. S.	C	15 Ga	Infirmity & poverty	G. W. Snellings	1862. Served 2 years. $60 1902-1905, 1909
Bromlee, J. W.		Beauregard Artillery	Age & poverty	A. S. Johnson, MD H. B. Harker, MD	1863 and served 9 months. $60, 1903-1905 Dead
Bryant, Wm.	F	3 Ga	Age & poverty	A. B. Smith N. G. Long, MD J. E. Johnson, MD	1864 and served to close of war. $60 1901-1905, 1909
Bailey, N. L.	G	37 Ga	Age & poverty	P. S. T. Bruce C. E. Earle, MD A. M. Tate, MD	1862 and served to close of war. $60 1902-1905, 1909

Name	Co	Regiment	Cause	Witnesses	Service and Amount Paid
Brough, W. H.	G	14 SC	Infirmity & poverty	J. L. Saxon N. G. Long, MD J. E. Johnson, MD	1861 and served to close of war. $60 1897-1898
Butler, J. F.	C	7 Ga	Age & poverty	R. M. Heard A. L. J. Stovall, MD A. J. Mathews, MD	1863 and served to close of war, 18 months. $60 1900-1905 Dead
Burriss, J. N.	B	34 Ga	Age & poverty	J. B. Childs J. Bryant, MD J. T. A. Gains, MD	1861. Discharged. $60 1897-1905 Dead
Beasley, W. Y.	I	44 Ga	Age & poverty	A. J. Bond A. J. Mathews, MD J. B. Bell, MD	1862 and served to close of war. $60 1897-1905, 1909
Bond, J. W.	H	38 Ga	Age & poverty	J. E. Campbell B. F. Smith, MD J. E. Johnson, MD	Served during war. $60 1897-1905, 1909
Bond, H. W.		3 Ga	Age & poverty	B. H. Oglesby N. G. Long, MD J. E. Johnson, MD	1864 and served to close of war, serving 7 months. $60 1896-1898 Dead
Bradford, J. M.	C	7 Ga	Age & poverty	A. M. Heard N. G. Long, MD A. J. Mathews, MD	1862 and served to close of war. $60 1896-1905, 1909
Broadwell, J. M.	F	15 Ga	Infirmity & poverty	J. J. Burch	1861 and served to close of war.

Name	Co	Regiment	Cause	Witnesses	Service and Amount Paid
					$60 1896-1905, 1909
Belcher, H.	A	1 SC	Infirmity & poverty		Served 4½ years. $60 1900-1903
Burden, J. J.	G	37	Age & poverty	W. B. Conway, MD Jno. Gerdine, MD J. E. Talmage	Served 12 months to close of war. $60 1902-1905, 1909
Bagwell, M. V.	C	16 Ga	Infirmity & poverty	H. B. Harper, MD A. L. Johnson, MD W. A. Mose	1863 and served to close of war. $60 1902-1904, 1909
Bond, W. H.	I	15 Ga	Infirmity & poverty	C. E. Earle, MD B. F. Smith, MD T. S. Gains	1862 and served to close of war. $60 1901-1902 Dead
Bullard, J. W.	C	7 Ga	Age & poverty		Served 3 years. transferred from Lincoln County. $60 1903 Dead
Brewer, J. M.	C	7 Ga	Age & poverty		1862 $0 1904, 1909
Bailey, L. L.	G	37 Ga	Infirmity & poverty	N. L. Bailey B. F. Smith, MD	1862 and served to 24 Apr 1865. Transferred Wilkes County 15 Jan 1906. Transferred to Wilkes County Mar 1908.

Name	Co	Regiment	Cause	Witnesses	Service and Amount Paid
					$60 1904, 1909
Bailey, R. B.	G	37 Ga	Infirmity & poverty		1862
Letter "B" carried forward to end of Roll					
Cosby, N. B.	C	15 Ga	Infirmity & poverty	J. L. Deadwyler, MD	1862 $60 1909
Cosby, D. C.	C	15 Ga	Age & poverty	N. B. Cosby	1861 $60 1904, 1909
Christian, J. W.	H	38	Disabled at Sharpsburg and detailed on guard duty in Atlanta, Ga.	Wm. Oglesby A. J. Mathews, MD	1861 and served 4 years. $60 1904, 1909
Chapman, W. B.		Corput;s Battery			$60 1904 Dead
Clark, E. V.	G	22 SC	Age & poverty		Served 2 years. $60 1904
Cofer, H. J.	C	1 Ga State Troops	Infirmity & poverty	A. J. Mathews, MD A. M. Tate, MD J. W. Smith	1864 and served to close of war. $60 1904 Died 1908
Christian, W. H.	H	Durrough's Battalion	Infirmity & poverty	A. L. J. Stovall, MD Jasper Bryan, MD A. Oglesby	1864 and served 7 months. $60 1900-1904
Colquit, J. H. P.		Toombs' & Pottle's	Infirmity & poverty	A. L. J. Stovall, MD C. E. Earle, MD	1863 and served 18 months.

Name	Co	Regiment	Cause	Witnesses	Service and Amount Paid
				J. W. Martin, MD	$60 1896-1899 Dead
Carpenter, F. N.	F	3 Ga	Infirmity $ poverty	N. G. Long, MD J. E. Johnson, MD J. A. Maxwell	1863 and served 8 months. $60 1898, 1903-1904
Cox, J. H.	H	3 Ga	Age & poverty	J. E. Cole, MD A. L. J. Stovall, MD P. E. Adams	1864 to 1865, served 7 or 8 months. $60 1904, 1909
Clark, W. H.	C	7 Ga	Age & poverty	A. L. J. Stovall, MD A. J. Mathews, MD B. D. Brown	1863 and served until sick, furloughed short while before surrender. $60 1903 Dead
Carpenter, W. H.	A	2 Ky	Age, infirmity, & poverty	B. F. Smith, MD J. E. Johnson, MD J. H. Brewer	1863 and served to close of war. $60 1901-1902 Dead
Cosby, J. M.	C	7 Ga	Infirmity & poverty	A. J. Mathews, MD J. B. Bell, MD J. M. Craver	1862 and served to close of war. $60 1901-1902 Dead
Craft, J. M.	A	2 Ky	Age & poverty	A. J. Mathews, MD J. B. Bell, MD W. H. Carpenter	1864 and served to close of war. $60 1900-1904, 1909

Name	Co	Regiment	Cause	Witnesses	Service and Amount Paid
Cox, W. C.	I	16 Ga	Infirmity & poverty	N. G. Long, MD J. E. Johnson, MD W. E. Simmons	1861 and served to close of war. $60 1901-1904, 1909
Colson, S. D.	C	15 Ga	Age, infirmity, & poverty	A. J. Mathews, MD A. L. J. Stovall, MD D. C. Cosby	1861 and served until discharged with lung trouble. $60 1901 Dead
Christian, C. F.	A	38 Ga	Infirmity & poverty	H. B. Harper, MD A. L. J. Stovall, MD A. Oglesby	1863 and served until wounded Sep 1864 & discharged. $60 1902-1903 Transferred Coweta.
Connell, J. D.	G	37 Ga	Infirmity & poverty	A. J. Mathews, MD A. B. Mathews, MD A. C. Fortson	1864 and served to close of war. $60 1902-1905, 1909
Craft, W. A.	F	15 Ga	Age, infirmity & poverty	L. P. Eberhardt, MD J. L. Christian, MD J. L. Deadwyler	1862 and served to close of war. $60 1903-1905, 1909
Clark, L. L.	F	15 Ga	Age & poverty	A. J. Mathews, MD A. B. Mathews, MD D. B. Alexander	1861 and served until resigned for disability, 12 months. $60 1903-1904 Dead

Name	Co	Regiment	Cause	Witnesses	Service and Amount Paid
Letter "C" carried forward to end of Roll					
Daniel, T. M.	K	3 Ga	Age & poverty	J. W. Goss, MD Jno. Gerdine, MD R. R. Reaves	May 1861 and served to close of war. $60 1901
Davis, H. S.	C	7th Ga	Age & poverty	J. B. Bell, MD A. L. J. Stovall, MD J. M. Brewer	1863 and served to close of war. $60 1897-1905 Dead
Dixon, A. W.	C	7 Ga	Age & poverty	A. J. Mathews, MD J. B. Bell, MD J. M. Corliver	Served 3 years. $60 1897-1905, 1909
Dickerson, E. J.	I	15 Ga	Age & poverty	J. E. Johnson, MD T. W. Bond, MD J. B. Alexander	1862 and served to close of war. $60 1899-1905, 1909
Dixon, S. W.	C	7 Ga	Infirmity & poverty	J. B. Bell, MD A. L. J. Stovall, MD J. W. Brewer	1863 and served to close of war. $60 1901-1905, 1909
Daniel, R. L.	K	2 Ga	Infirmity & poverty	A. L. J. Stovall, MD A. J. Mathews, MD D. C. Hunt	1862 and served to close of war. $60 1901-1905, 1909
Davis, W. P.	C	2 SC	Age, infirmity, & poverty	H. B. Harper, MD A. L. J. Stovall, MD J. A. Eaves	1861 and served until wounded, discharged Oct 1863. $60 1902-

Name	Co	Regiment	Cause	Witnesses	Service and Amount Paid
					1905, 1909
Dunn, Henry	C	16 Ga	Age & poverty	T. P. Eberhart, MD J. E. Johnson, MD G. Bailey	1861 and served until wounded at Spotsylvania & home 1865. $60 1902 to 1905. Transferred to Stephens County 1908.
Dobbs, D. M.	I	7 Ga	Infirmity & poverty	C. E. Earle, MD A. M. Tate, MD J. C. Reid	1861 and served to close of war. $60 1902-1904 Transferred to Fulton.
Denard, W. C.	K	1 Ga State Troops	Age & poverty		Served 11 months. Hart Transferred $60 1903-1905 Dead
Dixon, Abram					Transferred from Madison 6 Jan 1916 $60 1909
Deadwyler, J. L.	I	15 Ga	Infirmity & poverty	N. B. Cosby	1861
Eaverson, J. W.	F	38 Ga	Infirmity & poverty	A. L. J. Stovall, MD J. S. Christian, MD T. B. Thornton	1861 and served until wounded & discharged 1863. $60 1901-1905, 1909

161

Name	Co	Regiment	Cause	Witnesses	Service and Amount Paid
Fuller, J. J.		1 Ga	Age & poverty	C. Earle, MD A. L. J. Stovall, MD McAlpin Arnold	1864 and served to Mar 1865. $60 1896
Frost, W. F.	C	16 Ga	Infirmity & poverty	J. E. Johnson, MD N. G. Long G. Bailey	1862 and served until captured (1864) Elmira (1865). $60 1899-1905, 1909
Fortson, W. E.	I	15 Ga	Age & poverty	L. P. Eberhardt, MD A. S. Oliver, MD R. M. Willis	1861 and served to close of war. $60 1901-1905, 1909
Field, W. G.	F	22 SC	Age & poverty	A. S. Oliver, MD C. E. Earle, MD T. D. Thornton	1862 and served until in field hospital sick Apr 1865. $60 1903-1905, 1909
Faulkner, C. W.		Roswell Cavalry	Age & poverty		Spalding. $60 1903-1904 Dead
Fagan, L. M.	A	24 Ga	Age & poverty		1861. $60 1905 Dead
Fortson, M. E.	I	15 Ga	Infirmity & poverty	A. L. J. Stovall, MD N. Mattox	1861 to 9 Apr 1865. $60 1909
Fleming, J. H.	H	Toombs	Infirmity & poverty	R. E. Adams	1864. $60 1909
Gully, A. Y.	H	38 Ga	Age & poverty	J. E. Johnson, MD A. J. Mathews, MD	1861 and served 4 years. $60 1896-

Name	Co	Regiment	Cause	Witnesses	Service and Amount Paid
				W. H. Moon	1905, 1909
Galloway, Richard	I	15 Ga	Age & poverty	N. G. Long, MD J. E. Johnson, MD D. B. Alexander	1861 and served to close of war. $60 1902-1905, 1909
Ginn, W. P.	K	2 Ga	Age & poverty	A. S. Johnson, MD G. E. Daniels, MD T. J. Ginn	1863 and served to close of war. $60 1896-1900 Dead
Guest, S. D.	G	2 SC Rifles	Infirmity & poverty	J. B. Lewis J. E. Cole, MD	1862 and served to end of war. $60 1909
Gully, J. W.	H	38 Ga	Indigent	W. S. Parham J. T. Parham	Mar 1862. Transferred from Madison County 1909. $60 1909
Hall, Sam		14 SC	Age & poverty	A. L. J. Stovall, MD J. E. Johnson, MD J. E. Anderson	1861 and served until discharged 1862, sore leg. $60 1896-1905
Hill, L. M.	B	18 Ga	Age & poverty	F. L. Adams, MD A. L. J. Stovall, MD W. J. Beasley	1861 and served 4 years. Appomattox $60 1899-1905, 1909
Harper, J. E.		Toomb's Brigade	Age & poverty	A. J. Mathews, MD N. G. Long, MD J. W. Brewer	1863 and served to close of war. $60 1897-1900
Herring, I.	A	37 Ga	Age &	J. E. Cole, MD F. L. Adams, MD	1862 and served to close

163

Name	Co	Regiment	Cause	Witnesses	Service and Amount Paid
			poverty	W. J. D. Homes	of war. $60 1896-1898 Dead
Hendricks, A. E.	G	37 Ga	Age & poverty	A. L. Johnson, MD J. A. Dillashaw, MD W. B. Hendricks	1862 and served 3 years. $60 1899-1903 Madison
Hulme, Jno. D.	C	15 Ga	Infirmity & poverty	E. M. Bishop, MD B. F. Smith, MD T. S. Gains	1861 and served to 9 Apr 1865. $60 1898-1905
Hall, E. W.	H	37 Ga	Infirmity, age, & poverty		Served 2 years. $60 1902-1905
Hunt, S. J. W.	F	38 Ga	Infirmity & poverty	A. J. Mathews, MD J. E. Jenkins, MD J. C. Thornton	1862 and served 2 years until captured 1864 (Elmira, NY 1865) $60 1902-1905, 1909
Higginbotham, J. H.	K	4 Ga	Infirmity & poverty		Served 1 year. Transferred from Hart Jan 1906. Served 1 year. Hart $60 1903, 1909
Hamilton, H. F.	E	16 Ga	Infirmity & poverty	J. A. Thompson, MD J. G. Elder, MD J. D. Williamson	1864 and served to close of war. $60 1903-1905, 1909
Hilley, J. M.	G	Butler's SC	Infirmity &		1863 $60 1905,

Name	Co	Regiment	Cause	Witnesses	Service and Amount Paid
		Regiment	poverty		1909
Harper, Virgil E.	C	7 Ga Cavalry	Infirmity & poverty		1862 Transferred from Wilkes 1906. $60 1909
Hall, A. O.	D	7 SC	Infirmity & poverty	A. M. Shumate	1861 $60 1909
Hester, T. J.	I	15 Ga	Infirmity & poverty	J. L. Deadwyler	1861 $60 1909
Hammond, J. L.	K	16 Ga Cavalry	Infirmity & poverty	W. J. Gober C. M. Hammond	1863 and served to Apr 1865. $60 1909
Hewell, Thos. J.	H	38 Ga	Infirmity & poverty	W. A. Dexter G. A. Thornton	1862 and served to 3 May 1865. $60 1909
Jones, J. H.	I	15 Ga	Age & poverty	A. L. J. Stovall, MD Jasper Bryan, MD J. C. Booth	1861 and served to close of war. $60 1901-1905, 1909
James, A. A.	I	[smear] Ga	Age & poverty	N. G. Long, MD G. Y. Moore, MD R. M. Willis	1861 and served to close of war. $60 1899-1905, 1909
Jones, Nathaniel	D	9 Ga	Age & poverty	N. G. Long, MD A. J. Mathews, MD E. T. Caley	1864 and served to close of war. $60 1896-1897
Johnson, Jno. W.	F	2 Ga Cavalry	Infirmity & poverty	J. B. Eberhardt	$60 1909

165

Name	Co	Regiment	Cause	Witnesses	Service and Amount Paid
		Reserves			
Kidd, R. H.	E	38 Ga	Age & poverty	J. A. Dillashaw, MD H. B. Harper, MD Gully, A. Y.	1862 and served to close of war. $60 1901-1905, 1909
Kerlin, D. S.	C	15 Ga	Age & poverty	A. L. J. Stovall, MD J. E. Johnson, MD D. B. Alexander	1861 and served until wounded at Spotsylvania, on furlough 1865. $60 1904-1905
Kidd, James	D	1 Ga Reserves	Infirmity & poverty	W. M. McIntosh Thos. M. Swift	Served to Apr 1865. $60 1909
Lovinggood, S. J.	C	15 Ga	Age & poverty	J. D. Hulme W. M. Mathews	1861 and served to close of war. $60 1909
Lovinggood, G. W.	C	15 Ga	Infirmity & poverty	A. L. J. Stovall, MD J. B. Bell, MD R. M. Willis	1861 and served to close of war at Appomattox. $60 1900-1905
Lovinggood, W. L.	C	15 Ga	Age & poverty	A. L. J. Stovall, MD W. J. Mathews, MD J. P. Home	1861
McEwen, H. C.	D	16 Ga	Age & poverty	Jas. F. Payne W. B. Hadery	1863
Mattox, Clark	I	15 Ga	Infirmity & poverty	T. J. Hester	1861 $60 1909

Name	Co	Regiment	Cause	Witnesses	Service and Amount Paid
McIntosh, W. M.	D	1 Ga Reserves	Infirmity & poverty		1864 $60 1909
McIntosh, G. A.	B	7 Ga Cavalry	Age & poverty	R. M. Heard	1862 Died 1908
Moore, Joel W.	A	1 Ga Reserves	Infirmity & poverty	W. G. Cauthers	1863 $60 1909
Manning, J. J.	F	24 SC			1861 $60 1905
Moon, W. G.	H	38 Ga	Infirmity & poverty	H. B. Harper, MD A. J. Mathews, MD A. Y. Gully	1862 and served to 9 Apr 1865. $60 1900-1905, 1909
Moon, J. M.	C	15 Ga	Age, infirmity, & poverty	J. B. Bell, MD J. E. Johnson, MD R. M. Heard	1862 and served to close of war. $60 1900-1905 Died 1908
Maxwell, C. W.	H	38 Ga	Infirmity & poverty	H. B. Harper, MD A. L. J. Stovall, MD E. G. Bond	1862 and served 7 months, discharged with disability. $60 1905, 1909
Mathews, D. A.			Infirmity & poverty	A. L. J. Stovall, MD J. E. Johnson, MD J. J. Burch	1862 and served to close of war. $60 1896
Motts, W. A.	H & J	38 Ga	Infirmity & poverty	J. E. Johnson, MD A. C. Smith, MD E. B. Higginbotham	1862 $60 1896

Name	Co	Regiment	Cause	Witnesses	Service and Amount Paid
Morrison, Jasper J.	H	3 Ga	Age & poverty	A. J. Mathews, MD B. F. Smith, MD A. J. Mathews	1864 and served to close of war. $60 1896
Moore, Thos. A.	H	38 Ga	Age & poverty	A. L. Johnson, MD J. A. Dillashaw, MD A. M. Bowers	1861 and served to Appomattox. $60 1902-1905, 1909
Maxwell, J. A.	H	1 Ga	Age & poverty		Served 8 months.
Nash. R. C.	H	Toomb's Brigade	Age & poverty	J. B. Bell, MD A. J. Mathews, MD R. E. Adams	1863
Nash, S. J.		1 Ga	Age & poverty	J. E. Johnson, MD A. L. J. Stovall, MD W. J. Snellings	1864 and served to close of war.
Nash, G. T.	G	37 Ga	Age & poverty	A. J. Mathews, MD J. E. Johnson, MD E. P. Baily	1862 and served until captured, close of war.
Oglesby, Arda	H	38 Ga	Infirmity & poverty	J. R. Handsard J. E. Johnson, MD	1861 and served until captured at Spotsylvania & exchanged & under order received in company & served to end of war.
Ouzts, C. N.	K	14 SC	Age & poverty	A. L. J. Stovall, MD A. J. Mathews,	1862 and served to close

168

Name	Co	Regiment	Cause	Witnesses	Service and Amount Paid
				MD T. S. Gaines	of war.
Owens, F. E.	A	15 Ga	Infirmity & poverty	A. S. Oliver, MD J. B. Bell, MD Noah Scott	1862 and served until captured.
Owens, T. T.	K	20 Ga	Age, infirmity, & poverty	J. B. Bell, MD A. W. Mathews, MD F. E. Owens	1861 and served until captured.
Phelps, Thos.	D	1 Ga	Age & poverty	A. J. Mathews, MD J. E. Johnson, MD R. A. Burden	1864 and served to close of war.
Powell, J. F.	E	4th Reserves	Infirmity & poverty	J. D. Teasley A. J. Mathews, MD	1864 and served to close of war.
Pitts, D. Y.	A	6 SC Cavalry	Blindness & poverty	S. F. Bolt J. E. Johnson	1862 and served until captured.
Rhodes, G. B.	A	15 Ga	Age, infirmity, & poverty	J. E. Johnson, MD A. L. Oliver, MD J. D. Brewer	1862 and served to close of war.
Rice, A. M.	F	38 Ga	Age & poverty	A. L. J. Stovall, MD A. J. Mathews J. W. Hoyle	1862 to 1863.
Roberts, E. M.	C	15 Ga	Age & poverty	N. G. Long, MD J. E. Johnson, MD R. M. Willis	1861 and served to close of war.
Rowzee, T. F.	F	15 Ga	Age, infirmity, & poverty	J. E. Johnson, MD A. L. J. Stovall, MD J. L. Deadwyler	1861 and served to close of war.
Ridgway, J. T.	G	Confederate	Infirmity &	W. H. Christian	1864

169

Name	Co	Regiment	Cause	Witnesses	Service and Amount Paid
			poverty		
Roebuck, H. A.	C	Cobb Legion Cavalry	Age & poverty	Wiley C. Howard	1861 and served to close of war.
Sanders, W. G.	A	1 Ga	Infirmity & poverty	A. J. Mathews, MD N. G. Long, MD J. W. Moon	1864 and served to close of war.
Scoggins, W. D.	D	41 Ga	Age & poverty	J. A. Dillashaw, MD H. B. Harper, MD A. A. Seymore	1862 and served to close of war.
Shumate, H. M.	C	7 SC	Infirmity & poverty	J. E. Cole, MD J. B. Bell, MD T. S. Gains	1861 and served until disability 1863.
Simmons, W. C.	A	1 Ga	Infirmity, age, & poverty	A. L. Johnson, MD J. T. A. Gains, MD S. C. O'Kelly	1861 and served to close of war. Appomattox
Shaw, J. T.		Lumpkin Battery	Infirmity, age, & poverty	H. B. Harper, MD A. J. Mathews, MD U. R. Hodgson	1863 and served 14 months.
Smith, T. B.	C	15 Ga	Age & poverty	A. B. Mathews, MD A. J. Mathews, MD T. B. F. Willis	1862 and served until captured at Gettysburg 1863.
Stillwell, J. F.		32 Ga	Age & poverty	J. E. Johnson, MD C. E. Earle, MD Chas. Wesdorn	1862 and served to close of war.
Smith, Frank	F	15 Ga	Age & poverty	A. L. Johnson, MD H. B. Harper, MD	1861 and served to close

Name	Co	Regiment	Cause	Witnesses	Service and Amount Paid
				J. D. Gloer	of war.
Seymore, W. M.	I	15 Ga	Infirmity & poverty	A. J. Mathews, MD H. B. Harper, MD T. S. Gains	1862 and served to close of war.
Scott, W. T.	D	7 Ga	Age & poverty	A. L. J. Stovall, MD L. P. Eberhardt, MD J. M. Brewer	1863 and served to close of war.
James, J. H.					Dead 1909. $100 1890-1905, 1909
James, A. A.					Dead 17 May 1910. $50 1890-1892
Johnson, John N.					
Kidd, R. H.					
Kidd, James					
Lovinggood, S. J.					Died 6 Mar 1911.
Lovinggood, W. R.					Died 27 Jan 1917.
Mattox, Clark					Died 28 Feb 1915.
McIntosh, W. M.					Died [faint]
Moore, Joel, W.					Died 16 Jun 1913.
Moon, W. G.					Died 11 Jun 1912.

Name	Co	Regiment	Cause	Witnesses	Service and Amount Paid
Maxwell, C. W.					
Moore, Thomas A.					
Maybry, T. W.					Transferred Walton County 18 Aug 1911.
Outzs, J. M.					Died 16 Sep 1911.
Owens, F. E.					Died 3 Jan 1918.
Owens, T. T.					Died 4 May 1912.

1890-1909 Disabled or Invalid Soldiers Roll

The following table presents the transcribed information in six columns. The first column includes the name of the soldier, the second and third columns include the company and regiment or other unit in which the soldier served, the fourth column includes a description of the soldier's disability, the fifth column includes the names of the men who witnessed the pension application, and the sixth column includes the pension amounts paid and year of payment and all other information recorded by the clerk.

Name	Co	Regiment	Disability	Witnesses	Remarks and Amount Paid
Campbell, J. E.		37 Ga	Body wound 2nd Cold Harbor Mar 1864	D. B. Bell, MD M. P. Deadwyler, MD Geo. L. Almond	$50 1890-1905, 1909
Chasteen, A. C.	D	2 SC	Disabled arm Sep 1864		Madison $50 1896-1898 Franklin
Christian, J. W.	H	38 Ga	Disabled hand Sharpsburg, Maryland 17 Sep 1862	Jasper Bryan, MD B. F. Smith, MD J. E. Campbell	Transferred to Indigent List. $25 1890-1905
Colvard, R. N.		37 Ga	Lost finger Richmond, Virginia 27 Jun 1862		$5 1890-1905, 1909
Cofer, N. J.		14 Ga	Disabled arm Malvern Hill Jul 1862		Douglas $5 1899-1900 Troup
Chafin, J. C.	E	38 Ga			Transferred from Madison.
Dustin, W. J.					The record shows this party died 24

173

Name	Co	Regiment	Disability	Witnesses	Remarks and Amount Paid
					Jan 1900, paid widow 15 Feb 1900. No command given. $50 1899-1900
Dunn, Henry			3 fingers		$15 1900 Indigent
Duncan, J. W.	H	38 Ga	Lost finger Wilderness, Virginia 5 May 1864	M. P. Crowgler, MD H. B. Harper, MD T. D. Thornton	$5 1890-1891
Gaines, T. S.	I	15 Ga	Body wound Sharpsburg 17 Sep 1862	D. P. Bell, MD N. G. Long, MD R. M. Willis	$50 1890-1905, 1909 Died 9 Aug 1912.
Ginn, G. W.	H	38 Ga	Left arm disabled Spotsylvania 8 May 1864	I. G. Goss, MD J. A. Nabers, MD J. E. Campbell	$50 1891-1905, 1909
Ginn, Tinsley, J.	K	2 Ga	Wounds Jonesboro 31 Aug 1864	A. L. Johnson, MD J. A. Dillashaw, MD J. J. Jordan	$50 1903-1905, 1909 Died Nov.
Ginn, Thos. P.		Toombs' Brigade	Leg was amputated 1893. Horse fell on it.	I. G. Goss, MD Jasper Bryan, MD Geo. L. Almond	Does not know his company.
Hammond, A. E.	G	37 Ga	Disabled leg Atlanta, Ga. 22 Jul 1864	B. F. Smith, MD M. P. Deadwyler, MD Geo. L. Almond	$50 1890-1905, 1909

Name	Co	Regiment	Disability	Witnesses	Remarks and Amount Paid
Heard, R. M.	C	7 Ga	Left leg disabled McDowell's Farm 29 Sep 1864	J. A. Mathews, MD J. B. Bell, MD J. M. Brewer	$50 1890-1905, 1909
Higginbotham, E.	F	38 Ga	Lost both legs Spotsylvania Court House 12 May 1864	Geo. L. Almond	$150 1890-1905, 1909
Hill, J. M.	I	14 SC	Lost leg Gettysburg 1 Jul 1863	Geo. L. Almond	$100 1890-1905, 1909
Ingram, B. P.	A	59 Ga	Left leg disabled Gettysburg, Pennsylvania 2 Jul 1863	A. L. J. Stovall, MD N. G. Long, MD Geo. L. Almond	$50 1890-1891 Madison $50 1897 Madison $50 1899 Madison $50 1904 Died 1904.
Kinnabrew, E. N.	C	15 Ga	Disabled leg Spotsylvania 12 May 1864	J. J. Burch	$50 1896-1901 Dead
King, Geo. T.	E	43 Ga	Leg disabled Jonesboro, Ga. 31 Aug 1864	N. G. Long, MD Jasper Bryan, MD Geo. L. Almond	$50 1890
Lord, M. G.	E	34 Ga	Disabled arm 16 May 1863	B. M. Willis, Clerk Superior Court Acting Ordinary	Banks $50 1897-1898 Banks Dead
Mann, E. J.	H	38 Ga	Disabled leg Virginia 5 May 1864 Sheib		$50 1901-1905, 1909

175

Name	Co	Regiment	Disability	Witnesses	Remarks and Amount Paid
Oglesby, William	H	38 Ga	Right arm disabled Fredericksburg, Virginia 3 Dec 1862	Geo. L. Almond	Jones $50 1895-1905, 1909
Pulliam, William	H	58 Ga	Arm disabled 2nd Manassas	H. B. Harper, MD M. P. Deadwyler, MD Geo. L. Almond	$50 1890-1905 Dead
Porterfield, T. P.	A	4 Ga	Disabled arm Pine Mountain 7 Mar 1863	J. J. Burch	Oglethorpe $50 1898 Madison
Roberts, O. M.	H	38 Ga	Deafness, shell explosion near Richmond, Virginia Jun 1862	A. L. J. Stovall, MD N. G. Long, MD Geo. L. Almond	
Saxon, L. W.	D	10 Ga	Wound 6 Apr 1865 Virginia	J. E. Bell, MD A. L. J. Stovall, MD Jno. M. Brewer	$50 1900-1905, 1909
Sanders, C. H.	H	38 Ga	Lost leg Gettysburg 2 Jul 1863	Geo. L. Almond	$100 1890-1897 Dead
Shaw, A. J.		Echols' Artillery	Leg disabled Smithfield, North Carolina 10 Apr 1864	Geo. L. Almond	Cobb $50 1893-1895 Madison $50 1897
Simmons, W. J.	E	37 Ga	Lost leg Franklin, Tennessee Nov 1864	Geo. L. Almond	$100 1891-1902 Home
Smith, Frank			Lost finger Spotsylvania	A. L. J. Stovall, MD	$5 1890-1898

Name	Co	Regiment	Disability	Witnesses	Remarks and Amount Paid
			10 May 1864	N. G. Long, MD Geo. L. Almond	Indigent
Smith, F. W.	I	15 Ga	Disabled leg 2nd Manassas 30 Aug 1862	M. P. Deadwyler, MD B. F. Smith, MD Geo. L. Almond	$50 1890-1891
Terrell, J. B.	K	3 Ga	Lost one eye Kennesaw Mountain Dec 1864	N. G. Long, MD W. P. Deadwyler, MD Geo. L. Almond	$30 1890-1897 Indigent
Thornton, J. C.	F	38 Ga	Head wound Fredericksburg, Virginia Dec 1862	J. J. Burch	$50 1898-1905, 1909
Vaughn, A. W.	H	38 Ga	Right leg disabled Gettysburg 1 Jul 1863	B. F. Smith, MD Jasper Bryan, MD Geo. L. Almond	$50 1890-1904 Dead S. J. Vaughn for A. W. Vaughn lunatic.
Vickery, W. J.	B	24 Ga	Useless arm	W. F. Brown G. T. Cauthen S. M. Bobo	$50 1909
Wheliss, D. M.	C	15 Ga	Hand disabled Malvern Hill 1 Jul 1862	Geo. L. Almond	Oglethorpe $25 1895-1898 Indigent
White, J. L.	K	37 Ga	Left arm disabled Missionary Ridge Nov 1863	N. G. Long, MD B. F. Smith, MD Geo. L. Almond	$50 1890-1904, 1909
Willis, R. M.	C	15 Ga	Lost right leg North Anna, Virginia 23	Geo. L. Almond	$50 1890-1894 $100 1895-

Name	Co	Regiment	Disability	Witnesses	Remarks and Amount Paid
			May 1864		1900 Dead
Williams, W. A.	G	25 Ga	Right foot disabled Petersburg Jun 1864	Geo. L. Almond	Madison $25 1895-1897 Clarke

1909-1920 Indigent Soldiers Pension Roll

The following table presents the transcribed information in six columns. The first column includes the name of the soldier, the second and third columns include the company and regiment or other unit in which the soldier served, the fourth column includes the justification for granting the pension, the fifth column includes the names of the men who witnessed the pension application, and the sixth column includes the pension amounts paid and year of payment and all other information recorded by the clerk.

Name	Co	Regiment	Cause	Witnesses	Remarks and Amount Paid
Powell, J. F.					Died 18 Dec 1920. $60 1909-1916 $70 1917 $80 1918 $90 1919 $100 1920
Pitts, D. Y.					Died 19 Sep 1918. $60 1909-1916 $70 1917 $80 1918 $90 1919 Chk returned.
Rhodes, G. B.					11 Feb 1920 $60 1909-1916 $70 1917 $80 1918 $90 1919 $100 1920 Paid widow 1920.
Rowzee, T. F.					Died 3 Feb 1913. $60 1909-

Name	Co	Regiment	Cause	Witnesses	Remarks and Amount Paid
					1913
Ridgway, J. T.					Died 1915 in summer. $60 1909-1915
Roebuck, H. A.					Died 7 Dec 1914. $60 1909-1914
Smith, Jas. M.					Transferred from Oconee County 5 Dec 1911. Transferred to Clarke County 19 Nov 1912. $60 1912
Sanders, W. G.					Died 25 Aug 1918. $60 1909-1916 $70 1917 $80 1918
Shumate, A. M.					Died 19 Mar 1911. $60 1909-1911
Simmons, W. C.					Died 1909. $60 1909
Smith, T. B.					Died 5 May 1912. $60 1909-

Name	Co	Regiment	Cause	Witnesses	Remarks and Amount Paid
					1912
Stillwell, J. F.					Died 4 Oct 1913. $60 1909-1913
Smith, Frank					Died 19 Sep 1913. $60 1909-1913
Snellings, W. H.					Died 13 Nov 1910. $60 1909-1910
Smith, W. T.					19 Feb 1910. $60 1909-1912
Snellings, G. W.					$60 1909-1916 $70 1917 $80 1918 $90 1919 $100 1920
Snellings, G. T.					$60 1909-1916 $70 1917 $80 1918 $90 1919 $100 1920
Scoggins, J. W.					$60 1909-1916 $70 1917 $80 1918 $90 1919 $100 1920

Name	Co	Regiment	Cause	Witnesses	Remarks and Amount Paid
Smith, J. Willis					Died 16 Sep 1910. $60 1909-1910
Sanders, W. A.					$60 1909-1916 $70 1917 $80 1918 $90 1919 $100 1920
Smith, Jno. W.					Died 29 Jan 1913. Transferred from Wilkes County 3 Nov 1910. No record. $60 1911-1913
Terrell, J. B.					Died 15 July 1912. $60 1909-12
Thornton, M. J.					Died 8 Jun 1914. $60 1909-1914
Thornton, W. E.					Died 8 Oct 1911. $60 1909-1911
Tate, J. S.					Died 12 Jun 1913. $60 1909-1913
Thornton, J. C.					Died 4 Jul 1912.

Name	Co	Regiment	Cause	Witnesses	Remarks and Amount Paid
					$60 1909-1912
Turner, J. B.	B	1 Reserves	Infirmity & poverty	J. A. Teasley	Mar 1864 and served to Apr 1865 at Macon, Ga. Died 9 Apr 1917. $60 1910-1916 $70 1917
Tate, Jno. B.	D	1 Reserves	Age & poverty	Wm. McIntosh	Apr 1864 and served to Apr 1865 at Macon, Ga.
Wansley, Thomas N.					$60 1909-1916 $70 1917 $80 1918 $90 1919 $100 1920
Willis, J. S.					Died 20 Apr 1912. $60 1909-1912
Warren, D. H.					Died 13 May 1911. $60 1909-1911
White, A. L.					$60 1909-1916 $70 1917 $80 1918 $90 1919 $100 1920

Name	Co	Regiment	Cause	Witnesses	Remarks and Amount Paid
Willis, T. B. F.					$60 1909-1916 $70 1917 $80 1918 $90 1919 $100 1920
Webb, A. J.					Died 29 Apr 1917. $60 1909-1916 $70 1917
Young, J. C.					Died 2 Oct 1910. $60 1909

Law of 1910 Soldiers Pension Roll

The following table presents the transcribed information in six columns. The first column includes the name of the soldier, the second and third columns include the company and regiment or other unit in which the soldier served, the fourth column includes the justification for granting the pension, the fifth column includes the names of the men who witnessed the pension application, and the sixth column includes the date of enlistment, date and place of discharge or surrender, and the pension amounts paid and year of payment.

Name	Co	Regiment	Cause	Witnesses	Service and Amount Paid
Adams, W. H. H.	H	3 Ga		W. T. Kelley G. A. Lunsford C. T. Bond	May 1864 and served to Apr 1865 at Augusta, Ga. $60 1912-1916 $70 1917 $80 1918 $90 1919 $100 1920
Bringhurst, Ed S.	H	14 Tenn			Apr 1861 and served to Feb 1865. Transferred from Carroll County 11 Dec 1912. Mrs. Hartman, Pulaski County, Ark. $60 1913-1916 $70 1917 $80 1918 $90 1919 $100 1920
Blackwell, A. A.	H	3 Ga		R. E. Adams B. F. Harper	Died 17 Oct 1911. $60 1911
Caldwell, A. V.	C	15 Ga		N. B. Cosby W. A. C.	Aug 1862 and served to Apr

Name	Co	Regiment	Cause	Witnesses	Service and Amount Paid
				Hudson E. W. Nash	1865 at Appomattox Surrender. $60 1912-1916 $70 1917 $80 1918 $90 1919 $100 1920
Bailey, F. O.	F	15 Ga		M. E. Fortson T. M. Shumate E. S. Adams	July 1861 and served to Apr 1865 at Appomattox. $60 1913-1916 $70 1917 $80 1918 $90 1919 $100 1920
Gaines, W. P.	K	2 Ga		J. M. Harper C. B. Thornton	$60 1911-1916 $70 1917 $80 1918 $90 1919 $100 1920
Gaines, T. C.	G	15 Ga		M. E. Fortson T. J. Cordell	1861 and served to Apr 1865 at Appomattox. $60 1912-1916 $70 1917 $80 1918 $90 1919 $100 1920
Hardy, W. F.	K	18 Ga		T. M. Hill	$60 1911-1916 paid widow. Died 25 Dec 1915.
Hudson, W. A. C.	C	7 Ga Cavalry		T. S. Jones	$60 1911-1916 $70 1917 $80 1918 $90 1919

Name	Co	Regiment	Cause	Witnesses	Service and Amount Paid
					$100 1920
Hansard, J. R.	H	38 Ga		S. J. W. Hunt E. S. Adams	$60 1911-1916 $70 1917 $80 1918 $90 1919 $100 1920
Johnson, A. V.		Ferguson's Battery		Bryan Bauer D. A. McCall T. J. Mauldin	1863 and served until Reserve Guard 1 Mar 1865, all captured except. $60 1912-1916 $70 1917 $80 1918 $90 1919 $100 1920
Thornton, J. F.	G	3 Ga		J. L. Hewell L. L. Stovall	$60 1911-1916 $70 1917 $80 1918 Died 22 Feb 1918. Paid to widow.
Taylor, J. C.	F	15 Ga		N. B. Cosby R. W. Cleveland	Mar 1863 and served until Knoxville, Tennessee prisoner at surrender. $60 1913 Died 18 Apr 1913.
Hudgins, J. C.	G	62 Tenn		B. F. Billingsly, Moore Co., Tennessee McAlpin Arnold	Sep 1862 and served to Apr 1865. Wilkes County. $60 1913-1916 $70 1917 $80 1918

Name	Co	Regiment	Cause	Witnesses	Service and Amount Paid
					$90 1919 $100 1920 Died 30 Mar 1920. Burial expenses 1920
Reese, W. W.	E	16 Tenn Battalion		W. T. Caswell A. G. Lynch J. C. Higginbotham	Aug 1862 and served until New Charlotte North Carolina. $60 1914-1916 $70 1917 $80 1918 Died 7 Apr 1918
Butler, T. N.	H	38 Ga		W. G. Moon Geo. Haslett	Oct 1861 and served to 13 Mar 1865, Point Lookout. $60 1914-1916 $70 1917 $80 1918 $90 1919 Dead
Wood, Wiley	F	18 Ga		G. W. Mabrey	Aug 1862 and served to Feb 1965 at Fort Delaware. $60 1914-1916 $70 1917 $80 1918 $90 1919 $100 1920 Died 13 Oct 1913.
Fynch, A. G.	D	16 Tenn Cavalry		W. W. Reese Geo. Haslett B. E. Thornton	Sep 1862 and served to Apr 1865 at Washington, Ga.

Name	Co	Regiment	Cause	Witnesses	Service and Amount Paid
					$60 1913
Slay, G. F.	C	15 Ga		G. W. Snellings W. A. C. Hudson N. B. Cosby	Feb 1862 and served to 1865 at Richmond. $60 1914-1915 Dead
Eaves, J. A.	C	15 Ga		R. R. Leverdell F. O. Bailey R. G. Higginbotham	July 1861 and served until wounded, on furlough Feb 1865. $60 1914-1916 $70 1917 $80 1918 $90 1919 $100 1920
Fleming, Lawrence C.	D	1 Ga		T. M. Swift J. S. Lunsford T. A. Moons	Jun 1864 and served to Apr 1865 at Albington. $60 1914-1916 $70 1917 $80 1918 $90 1919 $100 1920
Oglesby, Wm.	H	38 Ga			Nov 1861 and served until returning Macon & Augusta, Ga. 4 Apr 1865. $60 1914-1916 $70 1917 Died 4 Mar 1917.

189

1909-1920 Indigent Soldiers Pension Roll

The following table presents the transcribed information in six columns. The first column includes the name of the soldier, the second and third columns include the company and regiment or other unit in which the soldier served, the fourth column includes the justification for granting the pension, the fifth column includes the names of the men who witnessed the pension application, and the sixth column includes the date of enlistment, date and place of discharge or surrender, and the pension amounts paid and year of payment.

Name	Co	Regiment	Cause	Witnesses	Service and Amount Paid
Burch, J. J.	F	14 Ga		F. O. Bailey E. A. Cason Geo. Haslett	Jul 1861 and served to Apr 1865 at Appomattox. $60 1915-1916 $70 1917 $80 1918 Died 27 Jun 1918.
Brown, J. R.	B	24 Ga		E. W. Philips, Hart County, Ga.	Aug 1861 and served to Apr 1865 at Appomattox. Ord 16 Apr 1917. $70 1917 $80 1918 $90 1919 $100 1920
Childs, J. B.	K	54 Ga		H. B. Osbons M. F. Moss J. J. Bulchin	Mar 1862 and served to Apr 1865 at Greensboro, North Carolina. $60 1915-1916 $70 1917 $80 1918 $90 1919 $100 1920

Name	Co	Regiment	Cause	Witnesses	Service and Amount Paid
Charping, W. L.	H	30 Ga		L. P. Hyatt S. N. Haley T. J. Cleveland	Apr 1864 and served to Apr 1865. $60 1916 $70 1917 $80 1918 $90 1919 $100 1920 Died 13 Jul 1921.
Hamm, P. H.	A	1 Missouri Cavalry		T. B. Crawford T. M. Swift J. T. Heard	17 Jun 1861 and served to 12 Feb 1865 at Point Lookout, smallpox at surrender. $60 1916 $70 1917 $80 1918 $90 1919 $100 1920
Heard, J. L.	G	9 Ga		W. B. Henny L. L. Bailey E. A. Cason	Mar 1862 and served until on sick furlough 1865. $60 1916 $70 1917 $80 1918 $90 1919 $100 1920
Hendrick, E. G.	H	38 Ga		E. B. Tate J. S. Campbell J. A. Ginn L. A. Rice	Apr 1862 and served to 9 Apr 1865 at Appomattox. $60 1916 $70 1917 $80 1918 Died 22 Dec 1917. Paid widow.

Name	Co	Regiment	Cause	Witnesses	Service and Amount Paid
Martin, P. C.	E	7 SC		A. O. Hall	Jan 1861 and served to Apr 1865 at Greensboro, North Carolina. $70 1917 $80 1918 $90 1919 $100 1920
Newton, J. B.	A	1 SC		Jno. W. Thomas of South Carolina	Apr 1862 and served to 15 Jun 1865 at Hart's Island, NY. No property. $60 1916 $70 1917 $80 1918 Struck from roll.
Sanders, T. W.					No record returned. Placed in 1916 by Commissioner Lindsey. $60 1916 $70 1917 $80 1918 $90 1919 $100 1920
Brooks, C. T.	G	25 NC			Feb 1864. Transferred from Hall County 2 Oct 1917. $80 1918 $90 1919 $100 1920

Name	Co	Regiment	Cause	Witnesses	Service and Amount Paid
Swift, T. M.	D	1 Ga Reserves		Jno. S. Tate J. Henry Thornton Walter M. Thornton	Apr 1864 and served to 1865 at Macon, Ga. $90 1919 $100 1920

1895-1909 Widows of Deceased Soldiers

The following table presents the transcribed information in six columns. The first column includes the names of the widow and her husband, the second and third columns include the company and regiment or other unit in which the soldier served, the fourth column includes the date and place of the husband's death, the fifth column includes the names of the men who witnessed the pension application, and the sixth column includes the date of enlistment, date and place of discharge or surrender, and the pension amounts paid and year of payment.

Name	Co	Regiment	Cause	Witnesses	Service and Amount Paid
Brown, P. E. w/o Asa C. Brown	F	38 Ga	Killed at Wilderness, Virginia May 1864	J. E. Campbell T. D. Thornton J. A. Bently	Mar 1862. $60 1895-1904 Dead
Bowers, A. E. w/o Elbert Bowers	A	19 Ga	Died Ashland, Virginia Hospital May 1862	G. L. Almond	Jun 1861. $60 1895-1904 Dead
Burden, E. C. w/o W. Burden	G	37 Ga	Died Newnan, Ga. disease	E. P. Bailey F. M. Gaines W. M. Adams	Mar 1862. $60 1895-1897 Dead
Booth, Elizabeth w/o J. R. Booth	A	1 Ga	Died at Atlanta, Ga. disease Jun 1864	J. W. Moore W. G. Sanders T. W. Sanders	Nov 1863.
Colvard, Marlin P. w/o Thos. Colvard	G	37 Ga	Died from disease Aug 1864	W. H. King T. N. Butler J. G. Seymore	Mar 1864. $60 1895-1904, 1909
Coker, Lottie E. w/o Jno. W. Coker	D	9 Ga	Died measles Jul 1862	E. P. Bailey J. L. Heard T. C. Burch	May 1862. $60 1895-1904 Transferred Fulton.
Cunningham, M. E. w/o Thos. C.	D	9 Ga	Died measles May 1862	F. M. Gains E. P. Baily	Mar 1862. $60 1895-

Name	Co	Regiment	Cause	Witnesses	Service and Amount Paid
Cunningham				J. A. Burden	1904, 1909
Colvard, Lucy A. w/o Jno. W. Colvard	D	1 Ga	Died disease Sep 1864	J. Y. Arnold J. F. Chandler R. A. Burden	Apr 1864. $60 1895 Dead
Dye, Ann H. w/o Joseph B. Dye	G	37 Ga	Supposed killed at Vicksburg, Mississippi 1863	T. C. Burch E. A. Baily J. A. Burden	$60 1895-1897 Wilkins $60 1899 Dead
Evans, Mary E. w/o William Evans	G	37 Ga	Killed Jonesboro, Ga. 1864	W. M. Adams E. P. Baily T. M. Gains	1862. $60 1895-1899 Dead
Fortson, S. B. w/o Jesser W. Fortson	F	38 Ga	Died disease Jul 1862	Abda Oglesby J. C. Thornton R. W. Cleveland	May 1862. $60 1895-1904, 1909
Graham, E. L. w/o Elijah Graham	H	34 Ga	Killed Jonesboro, Ga. Aug 1864	Jno. L. Cartledge M. L. McDonald A. M. Borders	May 1862. $60 1895-1903 Dead
Gaines, Frances P. w/o Jno. L. Gaines	B	24 Ga	Died Richmond Hospital Apr 1864	S. M. Bobo J. L. Johnson E. H. Sawers	March 1862. $60 1895-1904, 1909
Greenway, Mary A. w/o L. A. Greenway	F	38 Ga	Died disease Fall 1862 at Richmond	H. H. Pertain L. P. Pertain C. T. Dickerson	28 Jul 1862. $60 1895-1904 Transferred to Hart County 16 Apr 1908.
Ginn, Julia R. w/o J. A. Ginn	H	38 Ga	Killed Manassas	S. S. Ginn W. W. Kirby G. W. Ginn	Aug 1862. $60 1895-1904, 1909
Ginn, Mary F. w/o T. P. Ginn	H	Toombs'	Died Mar 1889.		Aug 1863. $60 1897-1904, 1909

Name	Co	Regiment	Cause	Witnesses	Service and Amount Paid
Harris, L. C. w/o David E. Harris		37 Ga	Died 9 Jul 1862		Mar 1862. $60 1899-1904, 1909
Hall, Mary E. w/o Linsley Hall	H	38 Ga	Died Apr 1863 measles	J. J. Burch J. T. Hansard J. E. Campbell	Aug 1862. $60 1895-1904, 1909
Hinton, F. W. w/o D. C. Hinton	B	24 Ga	Died 1864 disease	J. G. Seymore W. J. Teasley J. B. Terrell	Aug 1861. $60 1895-1904
Hewell, Martha A.	D	10 Ga	Died disease Aug 1863	E. C. Norman W. J. Ayers L. W. Saxon	Apr 1863. $60 1895-1904, 1909
Haynes, Sarah w/o B. F. Haynes	D	__ Ga	Died 12 Dec 1863 disease	G. Almond	$60 1895 Dead
House, Nancy T. w/o B. A. House	I	66 Ga	Died 1864 disease	Thos. Whitworth Willis Dudley J. T. Carrington	Sep 1863. $60 1895 Dead
Jones, M. L. w/o J. A. Jones	G	6 Ga	Died disease Jan 1866	J. J. Thomas E. Jones S. D. Linkton	Jun 1864.
Johnson, Mary P. w/o James Johnson					Madison $60 1897-1898 Madison
Jackson, A. O. w/o J. N. Jackson		34 Ga	Killed Jonesboro, Ga.	J. J. Burch	1862. Whitfield $60 1899 Whitfield
Jones, Lizzie w/o W. G. Jones	D	9 Ga	Died 17 Dec 1862 disease	R. M. Heard J. J. Burch A. E. Hammond	May 1862. $60 1895-1904, 1909 Died 9 Nov 1911.
Jordan, Mary J. w/o	F	38 Ga	Died 1869	F. M. Hendrick	Jul 1862.

Name	Co	Regiment	Cause	Witnesses	Service and Amount Paid
F. M. Jordan			consumption	J. D. Brown H. Moses	$60 1896-1904, 1909
Lovinggood, Susan E. w/o A. H. Lovinggood	D	7 Ga	Killed Mar 1864	J. M. Cosby J. M. Browner J. C. Thornton	7 Aug 1862. $60 1895-1896 Dead
Lewis, Mary A. w/o D. B. Lewis	C	16 Ga	Died Chattanooga, Tennessee 1864	G. L. Almond	Jul 1861. $60 1895-1896 Dead
Moon, Sarah w/o Jacob D. Moon	E	2 Ga	Killed or died from wound 28 Jun 1864	T. J. Ginn R. Rice J. J. Jordan	Sep 1863. $60 1895-1904, 1909
Maxwell, A. A. w/o W. H. Maxwell	F	38 Ga	Died 1864	R. M. Willis (acting Ordinary)	Mar 1862. Franklin $60 1897-1902 Dead
Mattox, E. M. w/o W. D. Mattox	B	1 Ga	Died Oct 1864 disease	J. N. Colquit T. H. Lumpkin R. M. Nard	May 1864. $60 1895-1897
Newbern, Ava w/o W. A. Newbern	G	37 Ga	Died Oct 1873	R. D. Brown S. A. Moore O. McCurry	Sep 1863. $60 1897-1904
Oglesby, Sarah F. w/o Thos. Oglesby	G	37 Ga	Died 15 Jun 1862 disease	Abda Oglesby E. T. Bailey D. P. Oglesby	Mar 1862. $60 1895-1904, 1909
Patton, Z. A. w/o Allen D. Patton		Echols'	Died 1883 consumption	C. W. Kidd J. H. Tiller R. H. Glenn	Mar 1862. $60 1897-1900 Clarke Oglethorpe $60 1904 Clarke
Parham, Sarah F. w/o Jno. W.	H	38 Ga	Killed 2 Manassas Aug	J. C. Booth C. M. Bard	Mar 1862. $60 1895-

197

Name	Co	Regiment	Cause	Witnesses	Service and Amount Paid
Parham			1862	J. G. Seymore	1904, 1909
Partain, H. E. w/o B. E. Partain	F	38 Ga	Died small pox Feb 1864	T. D. Thornton L. B. Partain H. H. Partain	May 1861. $60 1895-1904 Dead
Powell, Mariah w/o Wiley Powell	F	38 Ga	Died Lynchburg, Virginia 1864	W. M. Thornton J. D. Hulme T. D. Thornton	Jun 1862. $60 1895-1904, 1909
Powell, Millie w/o Noah Powell	D	27 Ga	Died 1899 on Roll in Wilkes County	D. H. Vernon W. M. Clark J. A. Brown	Mar 1862. $60 1896-1904
Pulliam, D. A. w/o Nathan Pulliam	H	38 Ga	Died 15 Mar 1865 disease	J. G. Seymore J. W. Booth W. S. Hall	Nov 1862. $60 1895-1899
Patton, Susan, w/o F. J. Patton	D	16 Ga	Died 18969 wounds	G. L. Almond	Jul 1861. $60 1895 Coweta
Pearson, Nancy w/o L. D. Pearson	F	38 Ga	Not heard of since war	J. C. Thornton A. Oglesby I. B. Almond	Feb 1862.
Peyton, E. C. w/o Jno. G. Peyton	H	38 Ga	Died measles 1862	J. C. Booth W. J. Brown A. W. Vaughn	Aug 1862.
Scoggins, Mary M. w/o Jno. J. Scoggins	K	6 Ga	Died disease 1862	J. L. Bridges W. E. Faugt J. T. England	May 1861. $60 1895-1900 Dead
Sanders, Mary A. w/o Jacob E. Sanders	H	38 Ga	Killed Gettysburg 1863	W. Pulliam A. J. Webb J. W. Bond, Sr.	Oct 1861. $60 1895-1904, 1909
Sorrow, R. J. w/o S. P. Sorrow	C	15 Ga	Died in hospital 1861	J. L. Deadwyler R. M. Willis G. W. Snellings	Jul 1861. $60 1895-1904 Dead
Smith, Mary E. w/o Jno. A. Smith	H	38 Ga	Killed Fishers Hill, Virginia	F. M. Hendrick G. W. Ginn	Sep 1861. 1895 Dead

Name	Co	Regiment	Cause	Witnesses	Service and Amount Paid
			1864	W. W. Kirby	
Smith, Almeta S. w/o Simeon Smith	B	1 Ga	Died in small pox hospital Oct 1862	G. L. Almond	Mar 1862.
Taylor, E. C. w/o J. J. Taylor	I	15 Ga	Died measles Apr 1862	C. T. Dickerson L. A. Gains J. D. Adams	1862 $60 1895-1904 Died 1908
Teasley, Mary B. F. w/o J. R. Teasley	H	Toombs'	Died disease 1863	W. B. Henry J. W. Norman J. W. Thornton	Sep 1863. $60 1895-1902 Dead
Thornton, L. A. w/o W. T. Thornton	F	38 Ga	Died from wounds Jan 1863	G. M. Campbell J. J. Arnold I. B. Almond	1862 $60 1895-1900 Dead
Thompson, M. E. w/o J. T. Thompson	D	16 Ga	Died Oct 1862 disease	G. L. Almond	Jun 1862. $60 1895-1896 Madison
Vaughn, Martha J. w/o Jacob D. Vaughn	H	38 Ga	Died Savannah, Ga. disease May 1862	J. G. Seymore E. M. Bond J. C. Booth	Oct 1861. $60 1895-1904, 1909
Whitaker, Mary w/o W. W. Whitaker	F	19 Ga	Died disease 19 Nov 1863 Winchester, Virginia	J. M. D. Stallings S. P. Burnett G. A. Gray	1862 $60 1895-1904, 1909
Whitman, Elizabeth w/o W. J. Whitman	F	24 SC	Killed Jackson, Mississippi May 1863	W. E. Shaw W. Evans J. M. Evans	Apr 1861. $60 1897-1904, 1909

1909-1920 Widows of Deceased Soldiers

The following table presents the transcribed information in three columns. The first column includes the name of the widow, the second column includes the pension amounts paid and the year of payment, and the third column includes the widow's post office address and all other information recorded by the clerk.

Name	Amount Paid	Remarks
Colvard, Martha P.	$60 1909-1916 $70 1917 $80 1918 $90 1919 $100 1920	Bowman, Ga.
Cunningham, M. E.	$60 1909-1916 $70 1917 $80 1918 $90 1919 $100 1920	Dewey Rose, Ga.
Fortson, S. B.	$60 1909-1916 $70 1917 $80 1918 $90 1919 $100 1920	Elberton, Ga.
Gains, Francis P.	$60 1909-1912	Died 9 May 1912
Ginn, Julia A.	$60 1909-1916 $70 1917 $80 1918 $90 1919 $100 1920	Bowman, Ga.
Ginn, Mary F.	$60 1909-1916 $70 1917	Died 12 Feb 1917. Returned
Harris, L. C.	$60 1909-1916 $70 1917 $80 1918	Died 8 Feb 1918. Returned Elberton, Ga.
Hall, Mary E.	$60 1909-1916 $70 1917	Died 7 Feb 1917. paid J. D. Hall invalid son.

Name	Amount Paid	Remarks
		Dewey Rose, Ga.
Hewell, Martha A.	$60 1909-1910	Died 7 Apr 1910. Dewey Rose, Ga.
Higges		
Jones, Lizzie	$60 1909-1911	Died 9 Nov 1911. Elberton, Ga.
Jordan, Mary J.	$60 1909-1916 $70 1917	Died 6 Nov 1917. Bowman, Ga.
Moon, Sarah	$60 1909-1915	Died Feb 1915. Elberton, Ga.
Oglesby, Sarah F.	$60 1909-1912	Died 1 Apr 1912. Elberton, Ga.
Parham, Sarah F.	$60 1909-1913	Died 21 Oct 1913. Elberton, Ga.
Powell, Mariah	$60 1909-1912	Died 26 Feb 1912 Elberton, Ga.
Sanders, Mary A.	$60 1909-1916 $70 1917 $80 1918 $90 1919 $100 1920	Elberton, Ga.
Vaughn, Martha J.	$60 1909-1910	Died 12 Aug 1910. Bowman, Ga.
Whitaker, Mary	$60 1909-1916 $70 1917 $80 1918 $90 1919 $100 1920	Bowman, Ga.
Whitman, Elizabeth	$60 1909-1916 $70 1917 $80 1918 $90 1919 $100 1920	Bowman, Ga.

1902-1909 Indigent Widows Roll

The following table presents the transcribed information in six columns. The first column includes the names of the widow and her husband, the second and third columns include the company and regiment or other unit in which the soldier served, the fourth column includes the date and place of the husband's death, the fifth column includes the names of the men who witnessed the pension application, and the sixth column includes the date of enlistment, date and place of discharge or surrender, and the pension amounts paid and year of payment.

Name	Co	Regiment	Cause	Witnesses	Service and Amount Paid
Adams, Sarah w/o James R. Adams	H	38 Ga	Age & poverty	A. S. Oliver, MD J. T. A. Gains, MD J. E. Campbell	1862 and served until captured Spotsylvania, prison 1865. $60 1902-1905, 1909
Adams, Elizabeth A. w/o Thomas J. Adams	E	38 Ga	Age & poverty	A. P. Johnson, MD J. S. Christian, MD J. L. Deadwyler	1861 and served until captured Gettysburg 1863. $60 1902-1905, 1909
Anderson, Permelia A. w/o W. A. Anderson	H	38 Ga	Age & poverty	A. S. Johnson, MD J. S. Christian, MD J. E. Campbell	1861, in prison at close of war. $60 1902-1905, 1909
Alexander, M. F. w/o T. R. Alexander	H	Toombs'	Age & poverty	N. G. Long, MD L. P. Eberhardt, MD S. Block	1864 and served until sick and furloughed Sep 1864. $60 1902-1905, 1909
Beasley, Mary E.	I	44 Ga	Was on indigent		$60 1905, 1909

Name	Co	Regiment	Cause	Witnesses	Service and Amount Paid
w/o W. T. Beasley			pension roll died 1905		
Bond, Nancy J.			Died 1902 before payment		
Brown, N. S. w/o T. J. Brown	G	37 Ga	Age & poverty	J. E. Johnson, MD T. W. Bond, MD E. P. Baily	1863 and served until captured Apr 1865. $60 1902-1905, 1909
Balchin, R. J. w/o Thomas Balchin	F	15 Ga	Age & poverty	W. J. Mathews, MD J. E. Johnson, MD L. S. Clark	Disability Jun 1862. $60 1903-1905, 1909
Burriss, Ann w/o J. N. Burriss	B	34 Ga	Infirmity & poverty	J. B. Jones, Jr. P. N. Burriss T. B. Tucker	$60 1909
Christian, C. H. w/o W. H. Christian	H	Durrough's Battalion	Infirmity & poverty	J. D. Gloer I. B. Gloer	Transferred to Madison County Dec 1908.
Clark, G. F. w/o W. H. Clark	C	7 Ga Cavalry	Age & poverty	B. D. Brown	$60 1909
Christian, Rachael w/o M. Christian	H	38 Ga		J. J. Burch	1862 to 1864. $60 1904-1905
Davis, Emily C. w/o T. S. Davis	C	7 Ga Cavalry	Was indigent pension roll, dead 1905		$60 1905, 1909
Faulkner, Henrietta w/o C. W. Faulkner		Roswell's Battalion Cavalry	Transferred Griffin, Ga.		1864 $60 1905

Name	Co	Regiment	Cause	Witnesses	Service and Amount Paid
Fagan, T. J. w/o L. M. Fagan	A	24 Ga	Indigent pension roll, died 1915		1861 $60 1905
Greenway, Mary w/o T. J. Greenway	H	Toombs'	Age & poverty	J. E. Cole, MD F. L. Adams, MD C. Mattox	1863 and served to Apr 1865. $60 1902-1904 Dead
Ginn, South R. w/o W. P. Ginn	K	2 Ga	Age & poverty	A. L. J. Stovall, MD H. B. Harper, MD J. J. Jordan	1863 and served 18 months. $60 1902-1905, 1909
Green, Callie C. w/o W. A. Green		Cuts	Age & poverty	A. L. J. Stovall, MD A. M. Tate, MD E. J. Edridge	1861 and served to April 1865. $60 1902-1905 Dead
Gray, Mary w/o T. L. Gray			Infirmity & poverty	N. L. Bailey Thos. M. Swift	1862 $60 1909
Haley, Mary E. w/o Willis Haley	K	2 SC			Served 5 months. $60 1909
Hull, Caroline R. w/o John W. Hull	F	Orr's SC	Age & poverty	C. E. Earle, MD A. L. J. Stovall, MD M. A. Terrell	1861 and served to Appomattox at close of war. $60 1902-1904 Transferred Hart.
Hall, T. A. w/o C. W. Hall	H	38 Ga	Infirmity & poverty	D. B. Maxwell R. E. Oglesby	$60 1909
Jones, Nancy A.	G	37 Ga	Age &	W. J. Mathews, MD	1861 $60 1903-1904

Name	Co	Regiment	Cause	Witnesses	Service and Amount Paid
w/o Nathan Jones			poverty	A. J. Mathews, MD E. P. Baily	Transferred Wilkes.
Kelley, Elizabeth w/o James Kelley	G	37 Ga	Age & poverty	W. J. Mathews, MD A. M. Tate, MD A. E. Hammond	1862 and served until disability 1864. $60 1903-1904 Dead
Little, Pennie w/o A. G. Little	F	50 Ga	Transferred from Franklin	W. Storms	$60 1905
Motes, Priscilla B. w/o W. A. Motes	F	38 Ga	Infirmity & poverty	J. E. Cole, MD F. L. Adams, MD T. N. Wansley	1862 and served until captured at Gettysburg, in prison at close of war. $60 1902-1905, 1909
Maxwell, Martha A. w/o G. M. Maxwell	G	61 Ga	Age & poverty	A. J. Mathews, MD A. B. Mathews, MD J. T. Erwin	1861 and served to 1863. $60 1903-1904 Dead
McDonald, Nettie w/o W. W. McDonald	H	34 Ga		J. J. Burch	1862 and served to Apr 1865. Fulton $60 1904-1905, 1909
Mattox, R. C. w/o W. H. Mattox	I	15 Ga	Age & poverty	Ches^r Mattox, A. S. Oliver, MD	1861 $60 1905, 1909
Moon, Martha F. w/o John S. Moon	H	38 Ga		W. S. Parham J. L. Baker, MD	Transferred from Madison 1909.

Name	Co	Regiment	Cause	Witnesses	Service and Amount Paid
					$60 1909
Oglesby, Mary L. w/o Abda Oglesby	H	38 Ga	Infirmity & poverty	M. J. Thornton A. J. Cleveland	$60 1909
Ramsey, Eliza J. w/o Archibald Ramsey	H	38 Ga	Age & poverty	B. B. Bell, MD C. E. Earle, MD J. E. Campbell	1861 and served until wounded and captured at Gettysburg. $60 1902-1904, 1909
Ramsey, Mary A. w/o Edmond Ramsey	G	37 Ga	Age & poverty	J. L. Christian, MD A. L. Johnson, MD J. A. Burden	1862 and served until captured Apr 1865 $60 1902-1904 Dead
Russom, M. A.					Transferred from Franklin County. 10 Mar 1908
Saxon, M. A. w/o A. J. Saxon	E	6 SC	Age & poverty	A. L. J. Stovall, MD A. J. Mathews, MD J. A. Hutchinson	Served to close of war. $60 1902-1904, 1909
Sanders, Mahulda w/o David M. Sanders					1902 died before payment.
Smith, Elizabeth M. w/o John J. Smith	F	Orr's SC	Infirmity & poverty	L. P. Eberhardt, MD B. F. Smith, MD B. F. Smith	1861 and served to Apr 1865. $60 1902-1904, 1909
Scarborough, C. W. w/o S. M.	E	37 Ga	Age & poverty	J. E. Johnson, MD C. E. Earle, MD	1863 and served to Apr 1865.

Name	Co	Regiment	Cause	Witnesses	Service and Amount Paid
Scarborough				J. J. Smith	$60 1903-1904, 1909
Thomason, L. E. w/o Hiram H. Thomason	K	1 Ga	Age & poverty	A. B. Mathews, MD A. J. Mathews, MD J. B. Terrell	1862 and served to close of war. $60 1902-1904
Terry, L. R. w/o Joseph Terry	F	38 Ga		J. J. Burch	1862 and served to Apr 1865. $60 1904, 1909
Tate, F. L. w/o Enos A. Tate	D	37 Ga 9 Ga Battalion	Infirmity & poverty	R. E. Adams D. P. Oglesby E. P. Bailey	$60 1909
Wheelis, S. E. w/o D. M. Wheelis	C	15 Ga		J. J. Burch	1862 and served to Apr 1865. $60 1904, 1909

1909-1920 Indigent Widows Roll

The following table presents the transcribed information in six columns. The first column includes the name of the widow and sometimes her husband, the second and third columns include the company and regiment or other unit in which the soldier served, the fourth column includes the justification for granting the pension, the fifth column includes the names of the men who witnessed the pension application, and the sixth column includes the date of enlistment, date and place of discharge or surrender, and the pension amounts paid and year of payment.

Name	Co	Regiment	Cause	Witnesses	Service and Amount Paid
Adams, Sarah					$60 1909-1916 $70 1917 $80 1918 Dead, Paid for funeral expenses. Died 31 Jan 1918. Elberton, Ga.
Adams, Elizabeth					$60 1909 Dead 1909. Bowman, Ga.
Anderson, Permelia A.					$60 1909-1912 Died 30 Jan 1912. Bowman, Ga.
Alexander, M. F.					$60 1909-1914 Died 7 Jan 1914. Elberton, Ga.
Adams, Elizabeth A. w/o Wm. R. Adams	K	3 Ga	Age & poverty	D. J. Maxwell J. H. Duncan	Hortense, Ga. $60 1910-1914 Died July

Name	Co	Regiment	Cause	Witnesses	Service and Amount Paid
					1914. Money returned. Elberton, Ga.
Beasley, Mary E.					$60 1909-1915 Died 17 Jun 1915. Elberton, Ga.
Brown, N. S.					$60 1909-1916 $70 1917 $80 1918 $90 1919 $100 1920
Balchin, R. J.					$60 1909-1916 Died 18 Oct 1916. Middleton, Ga.
Burris, Ann					$60 1909-1916 $70 1917 $80 1918 $90 1919 $100 1920 Heardmont, Ga.
Bell, R. C. w/o Dr. J. E. Bell	D	37 Ga			Transferred from Clarke County 21 Oct 1916. $70 1917 Died 14 Jul 1917.
Clark, S. F.					$60 1909-1912

209

Name	Co	Regiment	Cause	Witnesses	Service and Amount Paid
					Died Jun 1912. Elberton, Ga.
Christian, Lucy A. w/o John W. Christian	H	38 Ga	Age & poverty	J. E. Campbell J. W. Gully	$60 1910-1911 Died 1 Feb 1910. Bowman, Ga.
Craft, Rosa E. w/o W. A. Craft	F	15 Ga	Age & poverty	T. R. Rogers R. B. Galloway	$60 1911-1916 $70 1917 $80 1918 $90 1919 $100 1920
Davis, Emily C. w/o T. S. Davis	C	7 Ga Cavalry			$60 1909-1912 Dead 1911.
Ginn, Sarah R.					$60 1909-1916 $70 1917 Died Sep 1917. Bowman, Ga.
Gray, Mary				J. H. Higginbotham	$60 1909-1910 Died 30 May 1910. Middleton, Ga.
Higginbotham, Georgia w/o R. G. Higginbotham					$90 1919 $100 1920 Elberton, Ga.
Higginbotham, F. S. w/o E. B. Higginbotham	F	38 Ga			

Name	Co	Regiment	Cause	Witnesses	Service and Amount Paid
Haley, Mary E.					$60 1909-1910 Died 14 May 1910. Elberton, Ga.
Hall, T. A.					$60 1909-1912 Died 1911. Elberton, Ga.
James, Martha C. w/o A. A. James					$60 1911 Dead 1911.
Motes, Drucilla Z.					$60 1909-1915 Died 11 Apr 1915. Elberton, Ga.
McDonal, Nettie					$60 1911-1916 $70 1917 $80 1918 $90 1919 $100 1920 Died 7 Apr 1920. Burial Expense. Elberton, Ga.
Mattox, R. C.					$60 1911-1916 $70 1917 $80 1918 $90 1919 $100 1920 Elberton, Ga.
Mann, Martha F.					$60 1911-1913 Dead. Elberton, Ga.

Name	Co	Regiment	Cause	Witnesses	Service and Amount Paid
Oglesby, Mary L.					$60 1911-1916 $70 1917 $80 1918 $90 1919 Burial Expense.
Rousey, Eliza J.					460 1909-1910 Died 7 May 1910.
Rousey, Malinda w/o Mitchel Rousey	H	38 Ga	Age & poverty	J. W. Bond S. M. Bauer	Died Petersburg, Virginia 23 Oct 1863. $60 1910-1916 $70 1917 $80 1918 $90 1919 $100 1920 Dewey Rose, Ga.
Sanders, Alpha					Transferred from Hart County. $70 1917 $80 1918 $90 1919 $100 1920
Saxon, M. A.					$60 1909-1910 Died 16 May 1910. Elberton, Ga. J. C. Saxon
Smith, Elizabeth M.			Transferred to Dodge County 17		$60 1909-1916 $70 1917

Name	Co	Regiment	Cause	Witnesses	Service and Amount Paid
			Dec 1917		Transferred. Elberton, Ga..
Scarborough, C. W.					$60 1909-1916 $70 1917 $80 1918 $90 1919 $100 1920 Elberton, Ga. No 1 but self.
Smith, Peggy w/o Cleveland Smith					Transferred from Banks County 26 Dec 1911. $60 1912 Died 12 Dec.
Smith, C. E. w/o T. B. Smith	C	15 Ga	1910 Roll	N. B. Cosby	$60 1913
Terry, L. R.					$60 1909-1916 $70 1917 $80 1918 Dead. Elberton, Ga. Died 15 Apr 1918.
Tate, F. L.					$60 1909-1914 Died 1914. Elberton, Ga.
Terrell, P. A. w/o Jas. B. Terrell	K	2 Ga	1910 Roll	F. M. Haley T. D. Thornton	$60 1913
Thornton, S. E. w/o J. C. Thornton	H	38 Ga			$90 1919 $100 1920 Dewey Rose, Ga.

Name	Co	Regiment	Cause	Witnesses	Service and Amount Paid
Wheelis, S. E.					$60 1909-1912 Died 30 Aug 1912.

Law of 1910 Widows Roll

The following table presents the transcribed information in six columns. The first column includes the name of the widow and her husband, the second and third columns include the company and regiment or other unit in which the soldier served, the fourth column includes the date and place of the husband's death, the fifth column includes the names of the men who witnessed the pension application, and the sixth column includes the date of enlistment, date and place of discharge or surrender, and the pension amounts paid and year of payment.

Name	Co	Regiment	Cause	Witnesses	Service and Amount Paid
Burden, S. C. w/o R. A. Burden					$60 1911-1916 $70 1917 $80 1918 $90 1919 $100 1920
Burden, Frances E. w/o Thos. Burden					$60 1911 Died 9 Jun 1911.
Bond, Lucy C. w/o W. H. Bond					$60 1911-1916 $70 1917 $80 1918 $90 1919 $100 1920
Bates, Elizabeth w/o Elisha Bates					$6 1911-1914 Money returned. Died 29 Aug 1914.
Brown, S. C. w/o W. B. Bucker					16 Dec 1911 $60 1911-1916 $70 1917 $80 1918 $90 1919 $100 1920

Name	Co	Regiment	Cause	Witnesses	Service and Amount Paid
Clark, Sallie J. w/o Jas. L. Clark	D	15 Ga		B. D. Brown N. B. Cosby G. J. Hull	1861 and served until surrendered at Appomattox Apr 1865. $60 1911-1916 $70 1917 $80 1918 $90 1919 $100 1920
Cox, M. A. w/o W. C. Cox	F	16 Ga			Jul 1861. $60 1911-1916 $70 1917 $80 1918 $90 1919 $100 1920
Edwards, Georgia H. w/o E. P. Edwards	F	15 Ga		T. F. Rouzee George Haslett E. A. Cason	Jul 1861. $60 1911-1913 Died 28 Apr 1913.
Freeman, Mary M. w/o J. M. Freeman					$60 1911-1916 $70 1917 $80 1918 $90 1919 $100 1920 Burial Expenses. Died 1 Apr 1920.
Hairston, R. A. w/o J. C. Hairston	B	3 Ga Militia		M. V. Bagwell E. R. Goss	Sep 1863 and served until surrendered at Savannah, Ga Mar 1864. 16 Dec 1911 $60 1911-

Name	Co	Regiment	Cause	Witnesses	Service and Amount Paid
					1916 $70 1917 $80 1918 $90 1919 $100 1920
Goss, Cora A. w/o J. W. Goss					$60 1911-1916 $70 1917 $80 1918 $90 1919 $100 1920
Galloway, S. F. w/o R. B. Galloway					$60 1911-1916 $70 1917 $80 1918 $90 1919 $100 1920
Hammond, Mary F. w/o A. E. Hammond	G	37 Ga		D. P. Oglesby J. C. Thornton D. J. Thornton	1862 $60 1911-1916 $70 1917 $80 1918 $90 1919 $100 1920
Jones, Miley A. w/o Thos. Jones					$60 1911-1916 $70 1917 $80 1918 $90 1919 $100 1920
Jones, M. S. w/o J. H. Jones					$60 1911-1914 Died 12 May 1914.
Higginbotham, F. S. w/o E. B. Higginbotham	F	38 Ga		T. D. Thornton J. G. Seymour	$60 1913-1916 $70 1917 $80 1918

Name	Co	Regiment	Cause	Witnesses	Service and Amount Paid
					$90 1919 Died 30 Apr 1919.
Ray, Elizabeth w/o Sam Reynolds					$60 1911 Died 1 Dec 1910.
Seymour, S. w/o M. M. Seymour					$60 1911-1916 $70 1917 $80 1918 $90 1919 $100 1920
Scott, M. A. w/o J. C. Hudson				S. J. Lovinggood Geo. Haslett S. N. Haley	$60 1911-1916 $70 1917 Died 18 Jul 1917.
Smith, Jennie w/o J. Willis Smith	C	15 Ga			$60 1911-1916 $70 1917 $80 1918 $90 1919 $100 1920
White, L. M. w/o Robt. White					$60 1911-1916 $70 1917 $80 1918 $90 1919 $100 1920
Smith, Nancy E. w/o J. B. Smith	C	7 Ga Cavalry		B. D. Brown J. C. Thornton	Jun 1862. $60 1912-1916 $70 1917 $80 1918 $90 1919 $100 1920

Name	Co	Regiment	Cause	Witnesses	Service and Amount Paid
Snellings, Frances L. w/o W. H. Snellings	C	7 Ga Cavalry		T. J. Hewell, Jr. G. W. Snellings	$60 1912-1916 $70 1917 $80 1918 $90 1919 $100 1920
Thornton, Susan J. w/o Wm. E. Thornton	H	Toombs'		S. H. Jones E. D. Starks J. F. Thornton	$60 1912-1916 $70 1917 $80 1918 Died 5 Aug 1918.
Busby, Sallie H. w/o N. L. Busby	G	37 Ga		L. L. Busby W. A. Burden E. A. Cason	$60 1912-1916 $70 1917 $80 1918 Died 13 Mar 1918.
Burden, Nancy E. w/o Jno. J. Burden	C	37 Ga		W. Christian	On furlough Dec 1864. $60 1914-1916 Transferred to Telfair County 26 Dec 1916.
Bowman, A. E. w/o L. D. Bowman	C	7 Ga Cavalry		B. D. Brown	1863 $60 1914-1916 $70 1917 $80 1918 $90 1919 $100 1920
Brown, Martha A. w/o Jno. O. Brown	H	38 Ga		J. E. Campbell W. C. Burden C. V. Winn	May 1862 and served to Apr 1865 at Appomattox, Virginia $60 1914-

Name	Co	Regiment	Cause	Witnesses	Service and Amount Paid
					1916 $70 1917 $80 1918 $90 1919 $100 1920
Carpenter, H. D. w/o W. H. Carpenter	C	2 Ky Battalion		J. M. Craft G. G. Rennie	1864 $60 1912-1916 $70 1917 $80 1918 $90 1919 $100 1920
Cosby, B. A. w/o N. B. Cosby	C	15 Ga		L. L. Bailey T. M. Swift J. G. Ginn	$60 1915-1916 $70 1917 $80 1918 $90 1919 $100 1920
Craft, L. E. w/o J. M. Craft	A	2 Ky	Indigent		$60 1916 $70 1917 $80 1918 $90 1919 $100 1920
Smith, C. E. w/o T. B. Smith	C	15 Ga	~~On time. On 1910 Roll.~~	N. B. Cosby T. O. Taylor	$60 1913-1916 $70 1917 $80 1918 $90 1919 $100 1920
Cra					
Terrell, P. A. w/o Jno. B. Terrell	K	2 Ga		F. M. Haley	$60 1913-1916 $70 1917 $80 1918 $90 1919 Died 22 Jan 1919. Burial

Name	Co	Regiment	Cause	Witnesses	Service and Amount Paid
					Expenses
Taylor, M. E. w/o J. C. Taylor	F	15 Ga		R. P. Wood T. J. Cleveland J. A. Gully	$60 1914 Died 5 Mar 1914.
Booth, F. M. w/o Jno. C. Booth	E	38 Ga		W. N. Moore J. W. Brown L. J. Moore	Sep 1862 and served until Apr 1865 at Andersonville $60 1914-1916 Died 16 Aug 1916.
Eavenson, Frances Jane w/o George Eavenson	E	4 Ga		W. R. Ray D. J. Winn	Apr 1864. $60 1914-1916 $70 1917 $80 1918 Died 10 Jul 1918.
Hardy, M. E. w/o W. F. Hardy	K	18 Ga		W. L. [faint]	Gettysburg. $70 1917 $80 1918 Pd. 16 Apr 1917. Died 25 Aug 1918.
Adams, Parthenia J. w/o H. G. Adams	H	38 Ga		J. C. Thornton, Sr. J. A. Butler T. J. Maxwell	Oct 1861 and served to Feb 1865 $60 1914-1916 $70 1917 $80 1918 $90 1919 $100 1920
Anderson, Sarah A. w/o W. G.	I	15 Ga		T. M. Swift N. A. Carpenter	1865 Point Lookout. $60 1915-

Name	Co	Regiment	Cause	Witnesses	Service and Amount Paid
Anderson				G. G. Penner	1916 $70 1917 $80 1918 $90 1919 $100 1920
Adams, Sarah A. w/o M. B. Adams	G	37 Ga		R. L. Rice M. E. Maxwell	4 Mar 1862. $60 1915-1916 Died 3 Aug 1918. L. L. Baily
Hall, Lucy E. w/o James Hall	G	37 Ga		L. L. Busby J. A. Dillingham D. J. Pitts	May 1862 and served until captured 1864 Decatur, Ala., released 17 Jun 1865 Camp Douglas, Ill. $60 1914-1916 $70 1917 Died 3 Feb 1917.
Bowen, Annie E. w/o D. P. Bowen	I	1 SC		L. O. Busby G. A. Hall P. V. Rice	Dec 1864 and served until captured in hospital 13 Apr 1865 $60 1916 $70 1917 $80 1918 $90 1919 $100 1920
Wood, Elizabeth w/o Wiley Wood	F	18 Ga		Jno. R. White J. G. Seymour J. H. J. Vaughn G. A. Vaughn	$60 1915-1916

Name	Co	Regiment	Cause	Witnesses	Service and Amount Paid
Booth, L. C. w/o J. W. Booth	H	38 Ga			Oct 1861 and served until wounded at Fishers Hill 24 Sep 1864. Lost leg. $70 1917 $80 1918 $90 1919 $100 1920 Pd. 16 Apr 1917.
Pulliam, Martha J. w/o F. M. Pulliam	C & I	15 Ga		Clark Mattox, Sr. O. N. Owens J. M. Small	15 Jul 1861. $60 1916 $70 1917 $80 1918 Transferred to Hartwell 20 Dec 1918. Bowman, Ga.
Young, L. E. w/o J. C. Young	A	3 Ga		J. B. Gunter B. Gunter	$60 1912-1916 Died Summer 1916.

Certificate

The following certificate was inserted into the original record volume.

Georgia, Clarke County

I, the undersigned, do certify that Mrs. R. C. Ball, now of the County of Clarke, is the same person who as the Widow of Dr. J. E. Ball, Co. D, 37th Ga. Regt., Asst. Surgeon, pensioner was on the pension rolls of this county, and she drew a pension of Sixty dollars for 1916, and the bearer is same Indigent Widow (approved for 1916.)

Given under my hand and official seal of office Oct. 21st 1916

[Seal]   R. C. Orr [L. S.]

By her request transf'd to Elbert Co.

Law of 1910 Widows Roll

The following table presents the transcribed information in six columns. The first column includes the name of the widow and her husband, the second and third columns include the company and regiment or other unit in which the soldier served, the fourth column includes the justification for granting the pension, the fifth column includes the names of the men who witnessed the pension application, and the sixth column includes the date of enlistment, date and place of discharge or surrender, and the pension amounts paid and year of payment.

Name	Co	Regiment	Cause	Witnesses	Service and Amount Paid
Moss, Martha W. w/o W. A. Moss		3 Ga		D. J. Maxwell J. W. Pearson Propty J. R. Mattox B. L. Rode	1863 and served to 1865 at Augusta, Ga. New 1918 $80 1918 $90 1919 $100 1920
King, L. E. w/o W. H. King	G	37 Ga		L. L. Baily C. P. Hainton B. F. Ray	1863 and served until captured at Franklin, Tennessee Dec 1864 and released Point Lookout 26 Apr 1865. New 1918 $80 1918 $90 1919 $100 1920 Died 14 Apr 1919.
Moon, A. S. w/o W. G. Moon	H	38 Ga		T. N. Butler T. H. Butler J. L. Bragg	$90 1919 $100 1920
Thornton, Sallie C. w/o J. F. Thornton	G	3 Ga		J. M. Harper D. C. Hudson	$90 1919 $100 1920

Name	Co	Regiment	Cause	Witnesses	Service and Amount Paid
				C. J. Allmond	Elberton, Ga.
Hilley, Mary S. E. w/o J. M. Hilley	G	Butler's SC			1863 $100 1920 Elberton, Ga.
Fortson, Lucy J. w/o M. E. Fortson	I	15 Ga			$100 1920 Elberton, Ga.
Hewell, S. A. C. w/o T. J. Hewell, Sr.	H	38 Ga			1862 $100 Dewey Rose, Ga.
Brough, E. J. w/o W. H. Brough	G	14 SC			1861 $100 1920 Elberton, Ga. in South Carolina now.

Ex-Confederate Soldiers Living in Elbert County, January 1, 1923

The pre-printed form is titled *List of Ex-Confederate Soldiers Living in this, ___, County, January 1, 1923.* The following table presents the transcribed information in six columns. The first column includes the name of the soldier, the second and third columns include the company and regiment of other unit in which he served, the fourth column includes the date and place of the soldier's enlistment, the fifth column includes the date and place of the soldier's discharge or surrender, and the sixth column includes the soldier's post office address.

Name	Co	Regiment	Enlisted	Discharged	Post Office Address
Adams, S. A.	M	9 Ga Battalion	1865 Elberton	1865 Macon	Elberton
Adams, W. H. H.	H	State Troops	1864 Elberton	1865 Augusta	Elberton
Brown, D. P.	I	2 Ga Artillery	1861 Elberton	1865	Elberton
Brown, J. R.	D	24 Ga	1861 Hartwell	1865 Appomattox	Elberton
Brown, Jas. D.	H	38 Ga	1862 Elberton	1865 Appomattox	Bowman
Brown, B. D.	C	7 Ga Cavalry	1862 Elberton	1865 Greensboro	Elberton
Brown, A. G.					
Butler, T. N.	H	38 Ga	1861 Fort Lee	1865	Bowman
Bryan, Jasper					Elberton
Baily, L. L.	G	37 Ga	1862 Elberton	1865 Greensboro	Elberton
Bailey, F. O.	F	15 Ga	1861 Elberton	1865 Appomattox	Elberton
Caldwell, A. V.	C	15 Ga	1862 Elberton	1865 Augusta	Elberton
Cleveland, R. W.	I	15 Ga	1861 Elberton	1865 Appomattox	Elberton
Child, J. B.	G	24 Ga	1861 Cornelia	1865 Appomattox	Middleton

Name	Co	Regiment	Enlisted	Discharged	Post Office Address
Child, D. G.					Elberton
Cochran, T. W.					Elberton
Dixon, Abe	F	8 Ala	1861 Tallapoosa	1865 Roanoke	Elberton
Dixon, S. W.	C	7 Ga Cavalry	1863 [illegible]	1865 Fort Louis	Elberton
Dixon, Andrew	C	7 Ga Cavalry	1861 [illegible]	1865	Middleton
Davis, W. P.	K	2 SC	1861 Pickens, South Carolina	1865 Pickens, South Carolina	Elberton
Eavenson, J. W.	F	38 Ga	1861 Elberton	1865 Macon	Bowman
Fleming, J. H.	H	3 Ga State Troops	1864 Macon	1865 Fort Delaware	Middleton
Fleming, Lawrence	D	1 Ga State Troops	1864 Elberton	1865 at home	Elberton
Guest, S. B.	G	2 SC Reserves	1862 Anderson	1865 Elberton	
Gaines, P. C.	I	15 Ga	1862 Elberton	1865 Elberton	
Gaines, W. G.				Elberton	
Heard, E. B.	H				Middleton
Higginbotham, J. H.	H	4 Ga	Hart County		
Hudson, W. A. C.	C	7 Ga Cavalry	1863 Elberton	1865 Lookout Mountain	Elberton
Hamm, P. H.	A	7 Ga Cavalry	1861 Clinton, Mo.	1865 Point Lookout	Elberton
Hill, Thos. M.	B	18 Ga	1861 Conyers	1865 Point Lookout	Elberton

Name	Co	Regiment	Enlisted	Discharged	Post Office Address
Jones, J. M.	F	3 Ga	1864 Elberton	1865 Elberton	Elberton
Jones, F. A.	C	7 Ga Cavalry	1863 [illegible]	1865 Appomattox	Elberton
Johnson, A. V.			1865 Elberton	1865 Washington	Middleton
Johnson, J. N.	F	3 Ga	1863	1865	Middleton
Kelly, W. T.	I	3 Ga	1863 Elberton	1865 Augusta	Elberton
Mabry, J. W.	G		1863 Athens	1865 Elmira, NY	Elberton
Maxwell, Chandler	F	38 Ga	1861 Elberton	1865 Appomattox	Elberton
Mattox, N. M.	I	15 Ga	1861 Elberton	1865 Appomattox	Elberton
Maxwell, C. M.	H	38 Ga	1862 Elberton	1864	Elberton
Maxwell, Don J.					Elberton
Martin, P. C.					Dewey Rose
Norman, E. B.	I	15 Ga	1862 Elberton	1865 Appomattox	Elberton
Oglesby, D. P.	I	37 Ga	1862 Elberton	1865 at home	Elberton
Ray, W. R.	E	24 Ga	1864 Hartwell	1865 Lake City, Florida	Bowman
Roberts, W. C.					Bowman
Scarboro, W. T.	C	15 Ga	1864 Athens	1865 C. Charles	Elberton
Slay, G. F.	C	15 Ga	1863 Elberton	1865 Richmond	Elberton
Snellings, W. G.	D		1861 Elberton	1865 Appomattox	Elberton
Snellings, W. J.	D	1 Ga Reserves	1864 Atlanta	1865 Macon	Elberton
Smith, D. C.		64 Ga	1863 Atlanta	1865 Bentonville	Elberton

Name	Co	Regiment	Enlisted	Discharged	Post Office Address
Seymour, J. G.	H	38 Ga	1861 Elberton	1865 Appomattox	Dewey Rose
Sayer, J. W.		38 Ga	1864 Elberton	1864 Atlanta	Elberton
Sanders, W. A.		1 Ga State Troops	1863 Denmark	1865 Murphy	Elberton
Swift, T. M.	G		1864 Elberton	1865 home	Elberton
Smith, B. M.			1861	1865 Appomattox	Elberton
Thornton, T. D.				1865	Elberton
Thornton, J. W.				1865	Elberton
Tate, J. S.	C	15 Ga	1861	1865	Elberton
Teasley, J. A.	D	1 Ga State Troops	1865 Elberton	1865 Lake City, Fla.	Elberton
Tate, W. E.	G	3 Ga	1864 Elberton	1865 home	Elberton
Willis, Thos. F.		3 Ga	1862 Moon	1865	Elberton
Wansley, Thos. N.	F	30 Ga	1862 Hampton	1865 home	Elberton

Widows of Ex-Confederate Soldiers Living in Elbert County, January 1, 1923

The pre-printed form is titled *List of Widows of Ex-Confederate Soldiers Living in this, Elbert, County, January 1, 1923*. The following table presents the transcribed information in six columns. The first column includes the names of the widow and her husband, the second and third columns include the company and regiment of other unit in which he served, the fourth column includes the date and place of the soldier's enlistment, the fifth column includes the date and place of the soldier's discharge or surrender, and the sixth column includes the soldier's post office address.

Name	Co	Regiment	Enlisted	Discharged	Post Office Address
Adams, Mrs. Ann w/o J. R. Adams	F	36 Ga	1862 Elberton	1865	Elberton
Adams, Mrs. Cornelia w/o W. A. Adams	I	38 Ga	1862 Elberton		Bowman
Adams, Mrs. Sara E.					Bowman
Adams, Mrs. T. R. w/o T. R. Adams					Elberton
Anderson, Mrs. Sara E. w/o W. G. Anderson	I	15 Ga			Elberton
Adams, Parthenia					
Adams, Mrs. F. L.					Elberton
Bowman, Mrs. A. E. w/o L. D. Bowman		7 Ga Cavalry	1862		Middleton
Bowen, Mrs. A. E. w/o D. P. Bowen		1 SC	1864	1865	Bowman
Bond, Mrs. Catherine w/o	F	15 Ga	1862 Elberton	1865 Appomattox	Middleton

231

Name	Co	Regiment	Enlisted	Discharged	Post Office Address
W. H. Bond					
Burch, Mrs. Ida w/o J. J. Burch	I	15 Ga	1861 Elberton		Elberton
Bond, Mrs. Nancy E. w/o E. M. Bond					Dewey Rose
Brown, Mrs. N. S. w/o L. G. Brown	G	35 Ga			Elberton
Burriss, Mrs. Ann w/o J. N. Burriss	B	34 Ga			Elberton
Brown, Mrs. S. C. w/o W. B. Bucker					Elberton
Bond, Mrs. Lucy E. w/o W. H. Bond					Elberton
Cunningham, Mrs. M. E. w/o E. M. Cunningham		Ga Volunteers	1862 Elberton	1862 Knoxville	Dewey Rose
Booth, Mrs. L. C.					Elberton
Brown, Mrs. Martha A.					Elberton
Burden, Mrs. S. C.					Elberton
Chandler, Mrs. L. E.					Elberton
Charping, Mrs. S. E. w/o W. L. Charping					Elberton
Carpenter, Mrs. H. N. w/o W. H. Carpenter	F	15 Ga	1861		Elberton
Cox, Mrs. W. C. w/o W. C. Cox	I	15 Ga	1861 Elberton	1865	Elberton

Name	Co	Regiment	Enlisted	Discharged	Post Office Address
Craft, Mrs. W. A. w/o W. A. Craft	F	15 Ga	1862 Elberton	1865	Elberton
Cosby, Mrs. N. B. w/o N. B. Cosby	C	15 Ga	1861 Elberton	1865 Appomattox	Elberton
Craft, Mrs. L. E. w/o J. M. Craft					Elberton
Crawford, Mrs. M. L. w/o L. M. Crawford					Elberton
Carpenter, Mrs. H. N. w/o W. H. Carpenter		2 Ga Battalion		1864 surrender	Elberton
Cleveland, Mrs. M. E. w/o A. J. Cleveland					Elberton
Davis, Mrs. Emaline w/o T. L. Davis			1863 Elberton	1865 Elberton	Elberton
Daniel, Lou J. w/o W. A. Daniel	G	2 Volunteers	1861 Elberton	1865 home	Bowman
Fortson, Mrs. L. B. w/o Jesse Fortson	F	38 Ga	1862 Elberton	1865 Died	Elberton
Fortson, Mrs. M. J. w/o E. J. Fortson					Elberton
Ginn, Mrs. Mary					Bowman
Galloway, Mrs. R. B. w/o R. B. Galloway					Elberton
Goss, Mrs. Cora w/o Warren Goss		15 Ga	1862		Elberton
Ginn, Mrs. Julia					Bowman

233

Name	Co	Regiment	Enlisted	Discharged	Post Office Address
Higginbotham, E. E. w/o L. P. Higginbotham		38 Ga	1862	1865 Appomattox	Elberton
Hammond, Mrs. A. E. w/o A. E. Hammond	G	37 Ga	1862 Elberton	1865 home	Middleton
Hall, Mrs. T. A. w/o C. E. Hall	H	38 Ga			Bowman
Hilly, Mrs. L. E. w/o J. M. Hilly					Middleton
Hewell, Mrs. F. A. C. w/o T. J. Hewell					Dewey Rose
Jones, Mrs. Wilie w/o Thos. M. Jones	H	38 Ga	1864 Elberton	1865	Middleton
Jones, Mrs. M.					Elberton
Kinnebrew, M. E. w/o M. E. Kinnebrew	I	38 Ga	1861	1862 died	Dewey Rose
McIntosh, W. M. w/o Wm. McIntosh		Ga Reserves	1864	1865 Andersonville	Elberton
Mauldin, Mrs. Pernetta w/o T. J. Mauldin		15 Ga	1861		Elberton
McLanahan, Mrs. T. C. w/o Jos. McLanahan					Middleton
McCurry, Mrs. Susan B. w/o W. H. McCurry		3 Ga	1863		Elberton
Moss, Mrs. Martha w/o W. A. Moss					Elberton

Name	Co	Regiment	Enlisted	Discharged	Post Office Address
Maxwell, Mrs. L. M.					Bowman
Nash, Rachel F.			.		Elberton
Parham, Mrs. Dora w/o J. W. Parham	F	38 Ga	1862	1862 killed	Elberton
Rousey, Mrs. Melinda w/o Mitch Rousey	H	38 Ga			Dewey Rose
Rogers, Mary E.					
Seymour, Mrs. Sallie w/o N. M. Seymour		15 Ga	1861	1865 killed	Dewey Rose
Sanders, Mrs. Mary V. w/o John Sanders		38 Ga	1863 Elberton	Died	Dewey Rose
Smith, Mrs. W. T. w/o W. T. Smith		15 Ga	1865	1865	Elberton
Scarboro, Mrs. M. E. w/o S. N. Scarboro		37 Ga	1863		Elberton
Smith, Mrs. E. E.					Elberton
Smith, Mrs. Math E. w/o Jos. H. Smith					Elberton
Smith, Mrs. Nancy E. w/o J. B. Smith	C	7 Ga Cavalry	1862		Elberton
Sanders, Mrs. Alpha					Elberton
Smith, Mrs. Jennie					Elberton
Snellings, Mrs.					Elberton

Name	Co	Regiment	Enlisted	Discharged	Post Office Address
Frances L.					
Thornton, Sallie E. w/o J. C. Thornton	F	38 Ga			Elberton
Thornton, Mrs. S. E. w/o J. T. Thornton	G	3 Ga			Elberton
Warren, Mrs. Antoinette w/o John Warren					Elberton
Vickery, Mrs. L. E.					Elberton
Walker, Mrs. H. M.					Elberton
Willis, Mrs. E. A.					Elberton
Webb, Mrs. Mary E. w/o M. D. Webb					Elberton
Willis, Mrs. L. G. w/o R. M. Willis					Elberton
White, Mrs. Lucinda w/o R. A. White	F	38 Ga	1861 Elberton	1863 Fort Delaware	Elberton
Whittaker, Mrs. Mary	F	19 Ga	1862	1863 killed	Elberton
Whitman, Mrs. Elizabeth		34 SC	1861	1863	Bowman

Pensioners to be Paid Past Due Pensions

The following certificate heads the typewritten table of pensioners showing the past due pension payments amounts for the years 1922 through 1925.

Georgia, Elbert County

I hereby certify that the following list of names contains all of the Pensioners now in life and who are now residing in said County are on the Pension Roll of said County, and entitled to be paid the Pension due by the State of Georgia for any or all of the years ending December 31st, 1922, 1923, 1924, and 1925.

Given under my hand and official seal this 5 day of April 1926.

(Seal of Ordinary)

_____
Ordinary

Name	1922	1923	1924	1925	Total	Post Office
Widows						
Adams, Mrs. F. L.	150	75	75	60	360	Elberton, Ga.
Anderson, Sara A.	50	75	75	60	260	R. 2, Elberton
Bond, Nancy S.	150	175	75	60	460	R. I, Dewey Rose
Booth, Mrs. L. C.	50	75	75	60	260	R. I, Dewey Rose
Bowen, Annie E.	50	75	75	60	260	Bowman, Ga.
Brown, Martha A.	50	75	75	60	260	Bowman, Ga.
Bowman, A. E.	50	75	75	60	260	R. I, Middleton
Brown, N. S.	50	75	75	60	260	R. 7, Elberton
Burch, Ida J.	150	175	75	60	460	Elberton, Ga.
Burden, S. C.	50	75	75	60	260	Dewey Rose, Ga.
Burriss, Ann	50	75	75	60	260	Elberton, Ga.

Name	1922	1923	1924	1925	Total	Post Office
Carpenter, H. D.	50	75	75	60	260	R. 6, Elberton
Chandler, L. E.	150	75	75	60	360	Elberton, Ga.
Charping, Mrs. S. E.	150	75	75	60	360	Elberton, Ga.
Cosby, B. A.	50	75	75	60	260	Elberton, Ga.
Cox, M. A.	50	75	75	60	260	Elberton, Ga.
Craft, L. E.	50	75	75	60	260	R. I, Dewey Rose
Craft, Rosa C.	50	75	75	60	260	Elberton, Ga.
Fortson, M. J.	150	175	75	60	460	Elberton, Ga.
Galloway, S. F.	50	75	75	60	260	R. 9, Elberton
Ginn, Julia A.	50	75	75	60	260	Bowman, Ga.
Ginn, Mary	150	75	75	60	360	Bowman, Ga.
Goss, Cora A.	50	75	75	60	260	R. 6, Elberton
Hewell, S. A. C.	50	75	75	60	260	Dewey Rose, Ga.
Hill, Mrs. Fannie		175	75	60	310	#3 Hartwell, Ga.
Hilley, Mrs. S. E.	50	75	75	60	260	#1 Dewey Rose, Ga.
Jones, Miley A.	50	75	75	60	260	#1 Middleton, Ga.
Maxwell, L. M.	150	175	75	60	460	#6 Elberton
Mauldin, Permelia	150	175	75	60	460	#1 Middleton
Moss, Martha A.	50	75	75	60	260	Bowman
McLanahan, T. C.	150	75	75	60	360	Elberton
McMullan, J. L.	150	175	75	60	460	Elberton
Rogers, Mary E.	150	175	75	60	460	Elberton
Seymour, S.	50	75	75	60	260	Elberton

Name	1922	1923	1924	1925	Total	Post Office
Smith, Jenny	50	75	75	60	260	Elberton
Snellings, Frances L.	50	75	75	60	260	Elberton
Thornton, Sallie C.	50	75	75	60	260	#5 Elberton
Walker, H. M.	150	175	75	60	460	Bowman
Warren, Antoinette	150	175	75	60	460	Elberton
Webb, Mary E.	150	75	75	60	360	#5 Elberton
Whitaker, Mary	50	75	75	60	260	Bowman
Willis, E. A.	150	175	75	60	460	#1 Elberton
Willis, L. G.	150	75	75	60	360	Elberton
Stillwell, Lillie Dora				60	60	Elberton
Soldiers						
Adams, S. A.	150	175	75	60	460	#3 Elberton
Bailey, F. O.	50	75	75	60	260	#8 Elberton
Brown, S. C.	150	75	75	60	360	Bowman, Ga.
Bryan, Jasper	150	175	75	60	460	Dewey Rose, Ga.
Burden, J. A.	50	75	75	60	260	Comer, Ga.
Caldwell, A. V.	50	75	75	60	260	#7 Elberton
Childs, J. B.	50	75	75	60	260	#1 Middleton
Childs, S. G.	60	75	75	60	270	#1 Middleton
Cleveland, R. W.	50	75	75	60	260	Elberton, Ga.
Conwell, J. D.	50	75	75	60	260	Lavonia, Ga.
Davis, W. P.	50	75	75	60	260	Oglesby
Dixon, Abram	50	75	75	60	260	Elberton, Ga.

Name	1922	1923	1924	1925	Total	Post Office
Dixon, S. W.	50	75	75	60	260	Middleton, Ga.
Eavenson, J. W.	50	75	75	60	260	Bowman, Ga.
Fleming, J. H.	50	75	75	60	260	Middleton, Ga.
Gaines, P. C.	50	75	75	60	260	Elbertson, Ga.
Gaines, W. S.	50	75	75	60	260	Elberton, Ga.
Gulley, J. W.	50	75	75	60	260	Elberton, Ga.
Hamm, P. H.	50	75	75	60	260	Elberton, Ga
Heard, E. B.	150	175	75	60	460	Elberton, Ga.
Hudson, W. A. C.	50	75	75	60	260	#7 Elberton
Johnson, J. N.	50	75	75	60	260	Elberton, Ga.
Jones, J. M.	150	175	75	60	460	Elberton, Ga.
Kelley, W. T. Special	150	175	75	60	460	
Maxwel, Chandler	150	175	75	60	460	
Maxwell, C. W.	50	75	75	60	260	
Oglesby, D. P. Special	150	175	75	60	460	Elberton Loan & Savings Bk
Roberts, W. C.	150	175	75	60	460	
Slay, G. F.	50	75	75	60	260	
Snellings, G. W.	50	75	75	60	260	
Snellings, J. W.	150	175	75	60	460	
Swift, T. M.	50	75	75	60	260	
Tate, W. E.	150	175	75	60	460	
Teasley, J. A.	150	175	75	60	460	
Thornton, J. W.	150	175	75	60	460	

Name	1922	1923	1924	1925	Total	Post Office
Willis, T. F.	150	75	75	60	360	
Sanders, T. W.	50	75	75	60	260	

Index

242

Bridges
J. L., 198
Bringhurst
Ed S., 66, 74, 185
Broadwell
J. M., 24, 143, 155
Bromlee
J. W., 154
Brooks
C. T., 66, 192
Brough
E. J., 226
E. T., 89
W. H., 33, 155, 226
Brown
A. F., 44
A. G., 227
Asa C., 7, 194
B. D., 66, 74, 86, 140, 144, 158, 203, 216, 218, 219, 227
B. T., 24, 132, 150
B. W., 129
Ben D., 132
D. P., 227
E. W., 129
J. A., 198
J. D., 196
J. M., 40, 66, 138, 142, 154
J. R., 66, 74, 86, 132, 190, 227
J. W., 129, 221
James M., 132
Jas. D., 227
Jno. O., 219
John D., 132
John S., 140
L. G., 232
Martha A., 89, 98, 103, 109, 114, 118, 219, 232, 237
Mary E., 74
N. S., 19, 55, 57, 89, 98, 103, 109, 114, 118, 203, 209, 232, 237
P. E., 7, 194
R. D., 197
S. C., 89, 109, 215, 232, 239
S. G., 48, 50, 70, 74, 77, 80, 82, 86
S. W., 44

T. J., 203
Thos. J., 19
W. F., 123, 129, 133, 150, 177
W. H., 44
W. J., 198
Winnie A., 89, 109
Browner
J. M., 197
Brownlee
J. W., 133, 143
Jno. W., 38
Bruce
J. A., 44
P. S. T., 154
Bryan
Jasper, 70, 74, 77, 80, 82, 86, 129, 157, 165, 173, 174, 175, 177, 227, 239
Bryant
J., 155
Willis, 36
Wm., 154
Bucker
W. B., 215, 232
Buffington
R. T., 44
W. R., 44
Bulchin
J. J., 190
Bullard
J. W., 156
Burch
Ida, 232
Ida J., 55, 57, 60, 98, 103, 107, 109, 114, 118, 237
J. J., 132, 155, 167, 175, 176, 177, 190, 196, 203, 205, 207, 232
J. J., Sr., 130
T. C., 194, 195
Burden
E. C., 11, 194
Elizabeth, 62
Elizabeth P., 61
Frances E., 215
J. A., 48, 50, 52, 61, 74, 77, 80, 82, 86, 194, 195, 206, 239
J. J., 33, 134, 143, 156

J. W., 42, 141, 144
Jno. J., 219
Nancy E., 219
R. A., 169, 195, 215
S. C., 89, 98, 109, 114, 118, 215, 232, 237
Thos., 215
W., 194
W. A., 219
W. C., 219
Woodson, 11
Burger
  C. L., 150
Burnett
  S. P., 199
Burris
  Ann, 114, 119, 209
Burriss
  Ann, 89, 99, 109, 203, 232, 237
  J. N., 27, 155, 203, 232
  Joseph N., 133
  P. N., 203
Busby
  L. L., 219, 222
  L. O., 222
  Mary E., 24
  N. L., 219
  Sallie H., 219
  W. Y., 24
Bussey
  W. Y., 25
Butler
  J. A., 221
  J. F., 25, 155
  T. H., 225
  T. N., 66, 74, 188, 194, 225, 227
  Thomas N., 133
  W. S., 44
Cade
  Laura B., 107
Caldwell
  A. V., 67, 74, 77, 80, 82, 86, 137, 185,
    227, 239
Caley
  E. T., 165
Campbell
  G. M., 199

J. E., 26, 134, 151, 154, 155, 173, 174,
    194, 196, 202, 206, 210, 219
J. S., 191
Carpenter
  F. N., 158
  H. D., 90, 99, 103, 109, 114, 119, 220,
    238
  H. N., 232, 233
  N. A., 221
  N. S., 112, 115
  S. N., 55, 57, 60, 99, 103, 119
  W. H., 28, 158, 220, 232, 233
Carrington
  J. T., 196
Cartledge
  Jno. L., 195
Cason
  E. A., 190, 191, 216, 219
Caswell
  J. D., 34
  W. T., 188
Cauthen
  G. T., 177
  Geo. T., 129
Cauthers
  W. G., 167
Chaffen
  John C., 145
Chafin
  J. C., 43, 173
Chambers
  J. C., 141, 145
Chandler
  J. F., 195
  L. E., 55, 57, 60, 62, 99, 103, 107, 109,
    114, 119, 232, 238
Chapman
  J. W., 94
  W. B., 38, 39, 157
Charpin
  Willis L., 133
Charping
  S. C., 67
  S. E., 55, 57, 60, 62, 99, 103, 107, 110,
    114, 119, 232, 238
  W. L., 67, 107, 191, 232

246

J. A., 164, 166, 168, 170, 174
Dillingham
  J. A., 222
Dixon
  A. W., 26, 67, 75, 145, 160
  Abe, 228
  Abram, 42, 67, 75, 77, 87, 112, 146, 161, 239
  Andrew, 228
  Andrew W., 134
  Laura A., 100, 112, 119
  Mollie, 55
  Mollie S., 57, 60, 62, 99, 103, 112, 119
  S. W., 67, 75, 77, 87, 112, 134, 146, 160, 228, 240
  Sam, 26
Dobbs
  D. M., 161
Dudley
  W. J., 28
  Willis, 196
Duncan
  J. H., 208
  J. W., 174
Dunn
  Henry, 31, 161, 174
Dustin
  W. J., 173
Dye
  Ann H., 7, 195
  Joseph B., 7, 195
Earle
  C., 162
  C. E., 138, 154, 156, 157, 161, 162, 170, 204, 206
Eaton
  W. A., 146
Eavans
  Mary E., 14
  William, 14
Eavenson
  Frances Jane, 221
  George, 221
  J. W., 30, 48, 50, 52, 54, 67, 75, 78, 80, 82, 87, 228, 240
  Willis J., 135

Eaverson
  J. W., 146, 161
Eaves
  J. A., 160, 189
Eberhard
  L. P., 129
Eberhardt
  J. B., 165
  L. P., 159, 162, 171, 202, 206
Eberhart
  T. P., 161
Edridge
  E. J., 204
Edwards
  Clark, Jr., 68, 84, 85, 90, 93, 105, 106
  E. P., 216
  Georgia H., 216
  L. C., 127
Elder
  J. G., 164
Elgin
  W. D., 135
England
  J. T., 198
Erwin
  J. T., 205
Evans
  J. M., 199
  Jno., 14
  Mary E., 195
  W., 199
  William, 195
Fagan
  F. J., 24
  L. M., 24, 39, 162, 204
  T. J., 204
Falker
  C. W., 35
Falkner
  I. N., 45
Faugt
  W. E., 198
Faulker
  I. N., 45
Faulkner
  C. W., 23, 162, 203

249

250

251

252

257

259

Jno. W., 138
John, 23
Joseph, 207
L. R., 207, 213
Thomas
J. J., 196
Jno. W., 192
Thomason
H. H., 20, 138
Hiram H., 207
L. E., 207
Sallie, 20
Thompson
J. A., 164
J. T., 199
Jeremiah, 15
M. E., 15, 199
Thornton
B. E., 188
C. B., 91, 186
D. J., 217
G. A., 165
G. D., 129
J. C., 34, 43, 139, 152, 154, 164, 177,
182, 195, 197, 198, 213, 217, 218, 236
J. C., Sr., 221
J. F., 187, 219, 225
J. Henry, 193
J. T., 236
J. W., 49, 51, 52, 54, 72, 76, 79, 81, 83,
88, 199, 230, 240
L. A., 199
L. J., 125
Lucinda A., 9
Lucinda J., 93
M., 46
M. J., 38, 138, 154, 182, 206
S. E., 91, 97, 100, 111, 213, 236
Sallie, 102
Sallie C., 56, 58, 61, 63, 91, 97, 99, 111,
121, 225, 239
Sallie E., 236
Susan J., 219
T. B., 161
T. D., 72, 162, 174, 194, 198, 213, 217,
230

Tom, 91
W. E., 40, 139, 182
W. M., 198
W. T., 199
Walter M., 193
William T., 9
Wm., 125
Wm. E., 219
Tiller
J. H., 197
Tislin
C. C., 138
Treadwell
Perry, 138
T., 46
Tucker
T. B., 203
Turman
Jane E., 93
Turner
J. B., 183
J. W., 38
Jno. W., 139
Vardell
D. B., 130
Vaughn
A. W., 35, 177, 198
G. A., 222
H. D., 51, 52
J. H. J., 222
Jacob D., 10, 199
Martha J., 10, 199, 201
S. J., 177
Vernon
D. H., 198
Vickery
L. E., 93, 236
W. J., 152, 177
Walker
H. M., 56, 58, 61, 93, 97, 100, 102, 111,
121, 236, 239
O. A., 138
Wandley
Thos. N., 76
Wansley
T. N., 205

262

Thomas N, 183
Thos. M., 139
Thos. N., 69, 230
W. J., 46
Ware
    L. L., 130
Warren
    Antoinette, 56, 58, 61, 95, 97, 100, 102,
        108, 121, 236, 239
    D. H., 36, 139, 183
Wausley
    T. N., 25
Webb
    A., 137
    A. J., 42, 46, 140, 152, 184, 198
    J. C., 46
    M., 46
    M. D., 152, 236
    Mary E., 95, 100, 102, 108, 115, 121,
        236, 239
Wells
    T. B., 36
Wesdorn
    Chas., 170
Wheeler
    D. M., 17, 139
    S. E., 17
Wheelis
    D. M., 23, 207
    S. E., 23, 207, 214
Whelis
    D. M., 32
Wheliss
    D. M., 177
Whitaker
    Mary, 10, 91, 100, 115, 199, 201, 239
    W. W., 10, 199
White
    A. L., 36, 69, 140, 183
    J. L., 177
    Jno. R., 222
    L. M., 56, 58, 61, 63, 91, 95, 100, 115,
        119, 122, 218
    Lucinda, 236
    R. A., 236
    Robt., 218

T. R., 34, 139
Tinsley R., 46
Whitman
    Elizabeth, 10, 56, 91, 95, 100, 115, 119,
        122, 199, 201, 236
    W. J., 10, 199
Whittaker
    Mary, 236
Whitworth
    Thos., 196
Wilhite
    J. L., 31
Williams
    G. T., 46
    W. A., 178
    W. W., 46
Williamson
    J. D., 164
Willis
    B. M., 175
    E. A., 56, 95, 100, 108, 115, 119, 122,
        236, 239
    E. G., 95
    Elizabeth Ann, 69
    J. S., 139, 183
    Jesse, 29
    L. G., 57, 59, 61, 63, 100, 108, 115, 119,
        122, 239
    R. M., 162, 165, 166, 169, 174, 177, 197,
        198
    R. W., 139
    T. B. F., 69, 108, 140, 170, 184
    T. F., 49, 51, 53, 72, 76, 79, 81, 83, 88,
        241
    Thos. F., 230
Winn
    C. V., 219
    D. J., 221
Wise
    J. F., 26
Wood
    Elizabeth, 222
    J. M., 152
    J. W., 152
    R. A., 46
    R. P., 221

263